Andrew Brodie

Number Journey

for ages 10-11

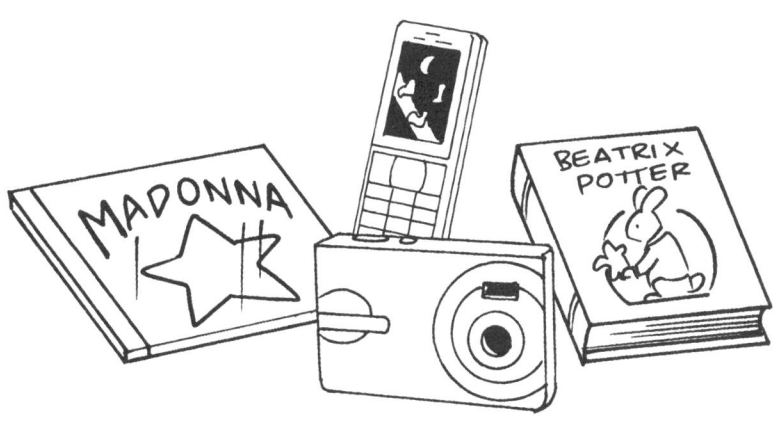

A & C Black • London

Contents

Introduction	3–4
Efficient written methods for addition	5–8
Efficient written methods for addition of decimals	9–12
Efficient written methods for subtraction	13–16
Efficient written methods for subtraction of decimals	17–20
Factors and prime numbers	21–24
Square numbers and prime numbers	25–28
Using multiplication facts to 10 x 10 to derive related multiplication facts involving decimals	29–32
Using multiplication facts to 10 x 10 to derive related division facts involving decimals	33–36
Using efficient written methods for the multiplication of a two-digit or three-digit number by a one-digit number	37–40
Using efficient written methods for the multiplication of integers and decimals by a one-digit number	41–44
Using efficient written methods for the multiplication of two-digit integers by a two-digit integer	45–48
Using efficient written methods for the multiplication of three-digit integers by a two-digit integer	49–52
Using efficient written methods for the division of integers by a one-digit number (Method 1)	53–56
Using efficient written methods for the division of integers by a one-digit number (Method 2)	57–60
Using efficient written methods for the division of numbers including decimals by a one-digit number	61–64

Andrew Brodie: Number Journey for ages 10-11 © A&C Black Publishers Ltd 2008

Introduction

Number Journey has been specially written to help teachers ensure progression in the teaching of number by addressing two key areas: the involvement of parents and the use of day-to-day assessment to promote success.

For many parents, the current methods used for teaching mathematics can be something of a mystery. Parents recognise certain aspects from their own school days but are surprised by some of the other approaches that are now being used in schools. The clash between the methods with which the parents are familiar and the methods their children are using in school can lead to many frustrations at home. The Williams review of 'Mathematics Teaching in Early Years Settings and Primary Schools' emphasises the role that parents can play in helping their children to learn mathematics. This can be summarised in the following four statements:

- Parents should be at the centre of any plan to improve children's outcomes.

- The panel heard time and again from children that they would like their parents to be taught the methods they are learning in mathematics, which have changed considerably since their parents were at school.

- The panel believes that the lack of clarification and setting out of the methods of teaching is a missed opportunity for engaging parents and improving their children's attainment.

- There is an opportunity for schools to work together with parents to dispel myths about the mystery of mathematics and give both children and parents a good grounding and positive attitude to this subject.

Number Journey addresses all four statements by providing materials that schools can use to ensure parents are given the opportunity to take an active part in their children's mathematical education. Current methods are explained clearly and the explanations are accompanied by activities that can be used at home to provide positive support for work at school. The teachers' notes for each unit specify clear learning objectives and list both outcomes and success criteria to enable teachers to make reliable assessments of pupils' work. The worksheets themselves are used to determine whether pupils have met the success criteria.

How is the book organised?

The materials in this book are organised into 15 units all designed to address the teaching of number – an area of maths in which many parents feel least confident but where they can actually be most helpful. *The Framework for mathematics teaching* includes a very wide range of learning objectives for understanding number, using number facts and calculating. In this book we have focused on the objectives where parental involvement will be most effective.

Each unit features an introductory page for teachers (*Teacher's Notes*), a letter for parents (*Help at Home Sheet*) that can be photocopied and sent home and two pupil worksheets (*Worksheets 1 and 2*). The calculation methods demonstrated on all the sheets are based on those recommended by the National Strategy.

Teacher's notes

These notes specify the learning objectives, learning outcomes and success criteria for each unit as well as suggesting opportunities for using and applying the skill being practised. The questions listed under 'Success criteria' are intended as prompts on which to base ongoing pupil assessment.

Help at home sheet

This is a letter for parents explaining what is being taught and, where appropriate, it also shows worked examples for parents to follow. There are also some ideas for relevant activities that can be completed at home. Introducing maths into everyday situations can increase a child's confidence and they can end up tackling complex number operations without even realising they are 'doing maths'.

Worksheets 1 and 2

The two worksheets provide activities that can be used by pupils for learning, for practising and for assessment. Where possible the children are encouraged to participate in their own assessment, identifying what they can do. Once a sheet is completed, discuss it with the child and help them to think about their own learning process. Ask questions such as 'How did you get on? Did you like this work? Did you find any of it too challenging?' With the second worksheet, discuss with the child whether they feel able to tick the 'I can' boxes. Celebrate their successes and support them if they are not ready to tick the boxes yet, by explaining that they will have another chance to revisit the concept and get more practice until they feel more confident.

Efficient written methods for addition

Teacher's notes

Building on previous learning
Before starting this unit check that the children can already:
- use efficient written methods to add and subtract whole numbers and decimals with up to two places. By Year 6, pupils are likely be familiar with the addition method shown in this unit, but it is provided here for revision and consolidation purposes while at the same time extending pupils' ability to deal with adding several numbers.

Learning objectives
- Use efficient written methods to add several whole numbers, including those with different numbers of digits.

Learning outcomes
The children will be able to:
- add sets of numbers together in columns.
- add numbers with different numbers of digits by writing them in the correct columns.

Success criteria
Can the children…
… complete the following additions in an efficient written form:
49 + 28 + 57, 92 + 15 + 67, 86 + 45 + 19, 78 + 33 + 45 + 29, 39 + 25 + 62 + 81, 81 + 56 + 98 + 34?
… complete the following additions in an efficient written form:
12 + 365 + 24, 6124 + 32 + 695, 7845 + 399 + 2764, 4093 + 318 + 27 + 695?

Resources needed
- A clear school policy on the systems and methods to be used in recording written addition.

Opportunities for using and applying the skills
- Solving multi-step problems, and problems involving fractions, decimals and percentages.
- Choosing and using appropriate calculation strategies at each stage, including calculator use. This book is concerned with calculation strategies based on mental work and written work. Calculators are not required for any of the activities in the book.

Pupils will probably have practised addition in the column method when they were in Year 5, looking at questions such as 589 + 356:

$$\begin{array}{r} 589 \\ + 356 \\ \hline 945 \\ {\scriptstyle 1\ 1} \end{array}$$

Questions in this unit will provide opportunities for pupils to revise this process and to extend it by considering questions such as 56 + 78 + 94 + 29, where there are several numbers to add together, and questions such as 574 + 68 + 273 + 4, where they will need to use their knowledge of place value to position the numbers correctly in the columns. More able pupils may like to look at each of the final two questions on Worksheet 1 and see if they can think of a number that can be multiplied by 4 to give the same answer as the addition shown.

Andrew Brodie: Number Journey for ages 10-11 © A&C Black Publishers Ltd 2008

Efficient written methods for addition

Help at home sheet

Child's name: Date:

Dear Parents
At school we follow the National Curriculum and the Primary Framework for mathematics. One aspect of our work in mathematics is the learning of number skills, including using efficient written methods for addition of whole numbers and decimals. The method that we demonstrate on this sheet is the traditional method of adding numbers in columns and 'carrying' numbers to the next column. Most pupils will have met this before in Years 4 and 5 but revision and consolidation of the process is essential. We are keen to involve parents in their children's learning so you may like to help your child by using some of the ideas on this sheet.

National Curriculum

The Primary Framework for mathematics says that Year 6 pupils should:
- use efficient written methods to add and subtract integers and decimals.

You could...

... practise additions with your child using the method outlined here e.g. to add together 4563 and 1247:

Step 1: Write the addition very neatly in columns ensuring that the units are in line above each other, and that the digits in the other columns are in line above each other:

```
   4563
+  1247
```

Step 2: Add the units and write the units part of the answer in the units column (in this case 0) and 'carry' the tens part of the answer to the tens column – encourage your child to write the carried number as small as possible.

```
   4563
+  1247
     ₁0
```

Step 3: Add the tens, not forgetting to add the one ten that was 'carried', and write the tens part of the answer in the tens column and 'carry' the hundreds part of the answer to the hundreds column, again writing it very small:

```
   4563
+  1247
    ₁1₁0
```

Step 4: Add the hundreds, not forgetting to add the one hundred that was 'carried':

```
   4563
+  1247
   8₁1₁0
```

Step 5: Add the thousands (note that nothing was carried from the hundreds to the thousands):

```
   4563
+  1247
  58₁1₁0
```

You may like to let us know how your child gets on with these activities – if so please return this sheet with any comments on the back.

Efficient written methods for addition

Worksheet 1

Name: _____

Date: _____

On this page I will be adding together sets of numbers.

I want to add together 68, 43, 27 and 36. This is how I can do it by writing it down:

Step 1: Write the addition in columns:

```
   68
   43
   27
 + 36
```

Step 2: Add the units to make a total of 24. The number 24 has 4 units and 2 tens so we write the 4 units in the units column and we write a tiny 2 in the tens column – some people call this 'carrying' the two tens.

```
   68
   43
   27
 + 36
   ₂4
```

Step 3: Add the tens and don't forget to add the extra two tens that you 'carried' so that you have a total of 17 tens. 17 tens are equal to 7 tens and 1 hundred so we write the 7 as the tens answer and 'carry' the 1 to the hundreds column. We don't need to write the 1 hundred very small as we can put it straight into position in the answer.

```
   68
   43
   27
 + 36
  17₂4
```

Try this method for answering the following questions. You will need to work them out in your maths book. It's very important to work tidily as you will make fewer mistakes.

Watch out! Sometimes you won't need to carry as there won't be enough units to make a ten or enough tens to make a hundred.

1. 49 + 28 + 57
2. 92 + 15 + 67
3. 86 + 45 + 19
4. 78 + 33 + 45 + 29
5. 39 + 25 + 62 + 81
6. 81 + 56 + 98 + 34
7. 63 + 12 + 59 + 38
8. 72 + 41 + 99 + 35
9. 99 + 88 + 77 + 66
10. 16 + 25 + 49 + 64
11. 30 + 31 + 32 + 33
12. 51 + 52 + 53 + 54

Efficient written methods for addition

Worksheet 2

Name: _____

Date: _____

I want to add together 6478 and 726.
This is how I can do it by writing it down:

Step 1: Write the addition in columns, making sure that the numbers are in the correct columns:

```
  6478
+  726
```

Step 2: Add the units, then the tens, then the hundreds, then the thousands, making sure that you 'carry' any numbers that you need to.

```
  6478
+  726
  7204
   ₁ ₁ ₁
```

Notice how important it is to write the numbers in the correct columns – the easiest way to do this is to always make sure that the units are in line in the units column. So, in the example above, the 8 and the 6 are in line in the units column.

Try this question:

```
  6794
   356
  2619
+   57
```

Use this method for answering the following questions. You will need to work them out in your maths book. It's very important to work tidily as you will make fewer mistakes. Remember to write the questions in columns and to keep the units digits in line in the units column.

① 12 + 365 + 24 ② 6124 + 32 + 695 ③ 7845 + 399 + 2764

④ 4093 + 318 + 27 + 695 ⑤ 56 + 989 + 2453 + 684 ⑥ 5225 + 148 + 4939 + 62

I can... I can add sets of numbers together in columns. ☐
I can add numbers with different numbers of digits by writing them in the correct columns. ☐

Andrew Brodie: Number Journey for ages 10-11 © A&C Black Publishers Ltd 2008

Efficient written methods for addition of decimals

Teacher's notes

Building on previous learning
This unit provides revision, for some pupils, in the process of adding numbers with decimals. For other pupils this aspect of maths will be new to them but they will be able to use their experience and knowledge of place value to learn the process effectively. Before starting this unit check that the children can already:
- explain what each digit represents in whole numbers and decimals with up to two places, and partition, round and order these numbers.
- use efficient written methods to add two-digit and three-digit whole numbers.
- use efficient written methods to add several whole numbers, including those with different numbers of digits.

Learning objectives
- Use efficient written methods to add integers and decimals.

Learning outcomes
- The children will be able to use efficient written methods to add integers and decimals.

Success criteria
Can the children…
… complete additions of money such as the following, in an efficient written form:
£149.50 + £12.25, £89.95 + £326.26 + £114.95, £39.49 + £6.48, £114.95 + £103.07, £149.50 + £6.48?
… complete the following additions in an efficient written form:
437.56 + 11.3, 69.08 + 5.3, 72.3 + 15.89, 16.4 + 3.89 + 25.72, 125.67 + 35 + 82.9 + 18.34?

Resources needed
- A clear school policy on the systems and methods to be used in recording written addition.
- Create a large number board to be used on the wall as a classroom display. It should consist of a grid of about ten rows with nine columns with the following headings: millions, hundred thousands, ten thousands, thousands, hundreds, tens, units, tenths, hundredths. Between the column headings for the units and the tenths there should be a very clear decimal point which should also be repeated between these columns on each row. Make some number cards to the back of which can be attached sticky-tack so that the cards can be positioned on the number board – or even better, use velcro on the backs of the cards and on the board. You will need approximately 4 copies of each digit from 1 to 9, and 10 copies of zero. Demonstrate some additions with the pupils, ensuring that they understand the positions of the digits in questions such as 4.2 + 3.49.

Opportunities for using and applying the skills
- Solving multi-step problems, and problems involving fractions, decimals and percentages.
- Choosing and using appropriate calculation strategies at each stage, including calculator use.
- This book is concerned with calculation strategies based on mental work and written work. Calculators are not required for any of the activities in the book.
- Represent and interpret sequences, patterns and relationships involving numbers: pupils will use their understanding of place value to carry out the repeating process of converting ten hundredths to one tenth, ten tenths to one unit, ten units to one ten, etc.
- Some addition of decimals may be completed in the context of money.

Andrew Brodie: Number Journey for ages 10–11 © A&C Black Publishers Ltd 2008

Efficient written methods for addition of decimals

Help at home sheet

Child's name: Date:

Dear Parents

At school we follow the National Curriculum and the Primary Framework for mathematics. One aspect of our work in mathematics is the learning of number skills, including using efficient written methods for addition of whole numbers and decimals. The method we demonstrate on this sheet is the traditional method of adding numbers in columns and 'carrying' numbers to the next column. Some of this work will be completed in the context of money. We are keen to involve parents in their children's learning so you may like to help your child by using some of the ideas on this sheet.

National Curriculum

The Primary Framework for mathematics says that Year 6 pupils should:
- use efficient written methods to add and subtract integers and decimals.

You could...

... practise additions of money with your child, using the method shown previously where we looked at adding four-digit numbers together.

For example, you could ask your child to find the total cost of a CD, a book and a bar of chocolate. Encourage him/her to write out the question like this:

```
   14.49
    5.99
+   0.65
---------
```
(Note that the price in pence has been converted to pounds: 65p = £0.65)

Explain to him/her that we have to add the right-hand column first. Note that this column is not the units because the units column is always before the decimal point. The question and answer will look like this:

```
   14.49
    5.99
+   0.65
---------
   21.13
   1 2 2
```
so the total price is £21.13

... give your child other questions using the four items shown above.

... give your child some questions based around your own shopping.

You may like to let us know how your child gets on with these activities – if so please return this sheet with any comments on the back.

Efficient written methods for addition of decimals

Worksheet 1

Name: _____

Date: _____

On this page I will be adding together money.

Answer the following questions in your maths book by writing the questions out in columns.

Find the total cost of:

1. a bike and a cycle helmet.
2. a digital camera, a television and a digital piano.
3. a mobile phone and a calculator.
4. a digital piano and a guitar.
5. a bike and a calculator.
6. a bike and a cycle lock.
7. all the items listed related to cycling.
8. all the items added together!

Andrew Brodie: Number Journey for ages 10-11 © A&C Black Publishers Ltd 2008

Efficient written methods for addition of decimals

Worksheet 2

Name: _____

Date: _____

I want to add together 12.69 and 8.2.

This is how I can do it by writing it down:

Step 1: Write the addition in columns, making sure that the numbers are in the correct columns. The easiest way to be sure is to check that the decimal points are lined up.

$$\begin{array}{r} 12.69 \\ +\ \ 8.2 \\ \hline \end{array}$$

Notice that there are no hundredths in the number 8.2 so that column stays empty, though some people prefer to write a 0 in it so that it could look like this:

$$\begin{array}{r} 12.69 \\ +\ \ 8.20 \\ \hline \end{array}$$

Step 2: Add the numbers together starting at the right-hand side in the hundredths column:

$$\begin{array}{r} 12.69 \\ +\ \ 8.20 \\ \hline 20.89 \end{array}$$

Try this method for answering the following questions. You will need to work them out in your maths book. It's very important to work tidily as you will make fewer mistakes.

① 8.6 + 3.4 ② 14.9 + 7.8 ③ 26.4 + 18.9

④ 37.56 + 11.3 ⑤ 69.08 + 5.3 ⑥ 72.3 + 15.89

⑦ 16.4 + 3.89 + 25.72 ⑧ 125.67 + 35 + 82.9 + 18.34

⑨ 206.04 + 315.63 + 18.29 + 71.5

I can... I can add numbers including decimals together. ☐

Efficient written methods for subtraction

Teacher's notes

Building on previous learning
Before starting this unit check that the children can already:
- Use efficient written methods to subtract whole numbers and decimals with up to two places. Note that in Years 3, 4 and 5 the children are likely to have developed a written approach to subtracting two-digit and three-digit numbers. This may match the method in this unit, decomposition, or it may have been complementary addition, or it could have been both methods. This unit provides revision of the process of decomposition.
- Every school should have a clear policy decision regarding the approaches to written calculations.

Learning objectives
- Use efficient written methods to subtract three-digit and four-digit whole numbers.

Learning outcomes
The children will be able to:
- subtract three-digit and four-digit whole numbers using the process of subtraction by decomposition.

Success criteria
Can the children…
… complete the following subtractions in an efficient written form:
547 - 329, 864 - 573, 700 - 235, 407 - 96, 817 - 378, 624 - 231?
… complete the following subtractions in an efficient written form:
8329 - 2714, 9876 - 3456, 2719 - 842, 7400 - 3865, 6248 - 2939, 8642 - 2987?

Resources needed
- A clear school policy on the systems and methods to be used in recording written subtraction.
- Dienes Base 10 apparatus if available. This apparatus provides excellent visual and physical clues for the process of written subtraction by decomposition. The children are able to use small cubes to represent units, sticks of 10 cubes to represent tens, square blocks of 10 tens to represent hundreds, and cube-shaped blocks of 10 hundreds to represent thousands. They can see that if they need extra units to subtract from, they can 'break' one of the ten sticks into ten units; if they need extra tens they can 'break' one of the hundreds into ten tens, etc.

Opportunities for using and applying the skills
- Solving multi-step problems, and problems involving fractions, decimals and percentages.
- Choosing and using appropriate calculation strategies at each stage, including calculator use.
- Represent and interpret sequences, patterns and relationships involving numbers: pupils will use their understanding of place value to subtract by decomposition. You may wish to start by reminding the pupils of the method, using a straightforward example such as 75 - 49. You could demonstrate this with Dienes apparatus if available, as well as in writing. The question is laid out in columns:

75
- 49

The first step is to subtract the 9 units from the 5 units. Clearly there are not enough so one of the 7 tens is broken into extra units, leaving just 6 tens in the tens column and giving 15 units in the units column:

$^{6}\cancel{7}^{1}5$
- 49

The child now subtracts the units then subtracts the tens:

$^{6}\cancel{7}^{1}5$
- 49

26

It would be worthwhile demonstrating a question such as 600 - 185. In this question a hundred will need to be broken into 10 tens, then one of those tens broken into 10 units, leaving 9 in the tens column, to be able to have enough units to subtract the 5.

Efficient written methods for subtraction

Help at home sheet

Child's name: _____ **Date:** _____

Dear Parents

At school we follow the National Curriculum and the Primary Framework for mathematics. One aspect of our work in mathematics is the learning of number skills, including using efficient written methods for subtraction of two-digit and three-digit numbers and beyond. The method that we are showing on this sheet is called 'decomposition'. Some pupils will have met this before in Years 4 and 5 but revision and consolidation of the process is essential. We are keen to involve parents in their children's learning so you may like to help your child by using some of the ideas on this sheet.

National Curriculum

The Primary Framework for Mathematics says that Year 6 pupils should:
- use efficient written methods to add and subtract integers and decimals.

You could...

... practise subtractions with your child using the method outlined here, with the example of 573 - 146:

$$\begin{array}{r} 573 \\ -146 \\ \hline \end{array}$$

The first step is to subtract the 6 units from the 3 units on the top line. Clearly there are not enough so one of the 7 tens on the top line is broken into extra units, leaving just 6 tens in the tens column and giving 13 units in the units column:

$$\begin{array}{r} 5\,\overset{6}{\cancel{7}}\,\overset{1}{3} \\ -146 \\ \hline \end{array}$$

Your child can now say '13 units subtract 6 units is 7 units, 6 tens (that's 60) subtract 4 tens (that's 40) is 2 tens (that's 20) and 5 hundreds subtract 1 hundred is 4 hundreds, so the answer is four hundred and twenty-seven.'

$$\begin{array}{r} 5\,\overset{6}{\cancel{7}}\,\overset{1}{3} \\ -146 \\ \hline 427 \end{array}$$

Here are some questions that you could practise with your child. He/she will need to work in a book or on a separate piece of paper and will need to lay each question out in columns, making sure that the numbers are in the correct columns. Tidiness helps to avoid mistakes. Notice that in some of the questions there is no need to get extra units from one of the tens because there are already enough units. In some questions your child will need to get extra tens by using one of the hundreds.

1. 683 - 192
2. 848 - 326
3. 984 - 236
4. 700 - 259 (clue: make some tens before making units)
5. 537 - 195
6. 823 - 369
7. 642 - 76
8. 712 - 356

You may like to let us know how your child gets on with these activities – if so please return this sheet with any comments on the back.

14

Andrew Brodie: Number Journey for ages 10-11 © A&C Black Publishers Ltd 2008

Efficient written methods for subtraction

Worksheet 1

Name: _____

Date: _____

On this page I will be subtracting three-digit numbers.

Look at this example: 625 - 397

Step 1: Write the question out very neatly in columns.

```
  625
- 397
```

Step 2: Look at the units first. We need to do 5 subtract 7, but 5 is not enough to subtract 7 so we use one of the 2 tens to make 10 extra units.

```
  6²¹5
- 397
```

Step 3: Now we can do 15 units subtract 7 units, which gives us 8 to put in the units part of the answer.

```
  6²¹5
- 397
     8
```

Step 4: Now we have 1 ten to subtract 9 tens. Again this is not enough so we use one of the 6 hundreds to make 10 extra tens, giving us 11 tens to subtract the 9 tens and 5 hundreds to subtract the 3 hundreds.

```
  ⁵⁶¹¹²¹5
- 3 9 7
  2 2 8
```

Use this method to answer the questions below. You will need to work neatly in your maths book or on a separate piece of paper. Remember to always check whether you need extra units or extra tens. Sometimes you will have enough. Sometimes you will need to break a hundred into 10 tens then break one of these tens into 10 units.

① 694 - 237   ② 906 - 555   ③ 658 - 132

④ 547 - 329   ⑤ 864 - 573   ⑥ 700 - 235

⑦ 407 - 96   ⑧ 817 - 378   ⑨ 624 - 231

⑩ 956 - 88   ⑪ 781 - 199   ⑫ 567 - 398

Andrew Brodie: Number Journey for ages 10-11 © A&C Black Publishers Ltd 2008

Efficient written methods for subtraction

Worksheet 2

Name: _____

Date: _____

Find the subtractions from 6000. You may need to do some calculations in your book or on a separate piece of paper.

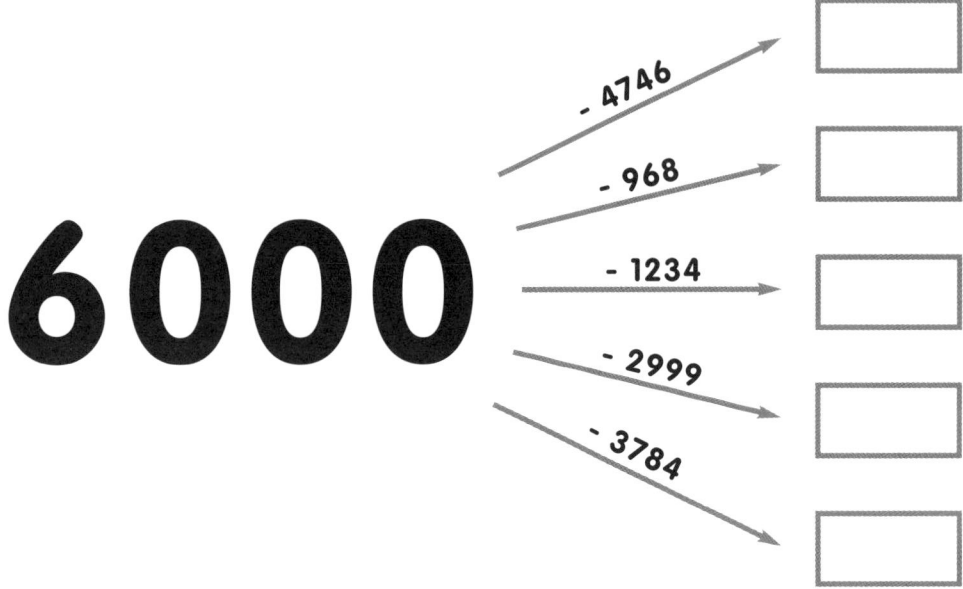

Now complete the following subtractions in your maths book. Work very neatly as you are less likely to make mistakes.

1. 8329 - 2714
2. 9876 - 3456
3. 2719 - 842
4. 7400 - 3865
5. 6248 - 2939
6. 8642 - 2987

I can...
I can subtract three-digit numbers. ☐
I can subtract four-digit numbers. ☐

Andrew Brodie: Number Journey for ages 10-11 © A&C Black Publishers Ltd 2008

Efficient written methods for subtraction of decimals

Teacher's notes

Building on previous learning
- Before starting this unit check that the children can already:
- Use efficient written methods to subtract whole numbers and decimals with up to two places. Note that in Years 3, 4 and 5 the children are likely to have developed a written approach to subtracting two-digit and three-digit numbers – this may match the method in this unit, decomposition, or it may have been complementary addition, or it could have been both methods. This unit provides revision of the process of decomposition, applying the process to the subtraction of decimals.
- Every school should have a clear policy decision regarding the approaches to written calculations.

Learning objectives
- Use efficient written methods to subtract integers and decimals.

Learning outcomes
- The children will be able to subtract integers and decimals using the process of subtraction by decomposition.
- The children will know the term 'integer'.

Success criteria
Can the children…
… complete the following subtractions in an efficient written form:
733 - 289, 854 - 539, 492 - 186, 829 - 364, 750 - 399, 999 - 357?
… complete the following subtractions in an efficient written form:
8 - 1.84, 9.01 - 3.59, 10 - 2.65, 8.69 - 3.9, 15 - 6.04, 17.9 - 5.86?

Resources needed
- A clear school policy on the systems and methods to be used in recording written subtraction.
- Create a large number board to be used on the wall as a classroom display (see page 9 for details).

Opportunities for using and applying the skills
- Solving multi-step problems, and problems involving fractions, decimals and percentages.
- Choosing and using appropriate calculation strategies at each stage, including calculator use. This book is concerned with calculation strategies based on mental work and written work. Calculators are not required for any of the activities in the book.
- Represent and interpret sequences, patterns and relationships involving numbers: pupils will use their understanding of place value to subtract by decomposition.
- You could use your number board to demonstrate some subtractions with the pupils, ensuring that they understand the positions of the digits in questions such as 4.2 - 3.49.

Efficient written methods for subtraction of decimals

Help at home sheet

Child's name: **Date:**

Dear Parents

At school we follow the National Curriculum and the Primary Framework for mathematics. One aspect of our work in mathematics is the learning of number skills, including using efficient written methods for subtraction of whole numbers and decimals. The method that we are showing on this sheet is called 'decomposition' and you will already have seen this method in use for subtraction of whole numbers. We are keen to involve parents in their children's learning so you may like to help your child by using some of the ideas on this sheet.

National Curriculum

The Primary Framework for Mathematics says that Year 6 pupils should:
- use efficient written methods to add and subtract integers and decimals.

You could...

… practise subtractions with your child using the method outlined here, with the example of 98.4 - 34.6:

   98.4
  -34.6

The first step is to subtract the 6 tenths from the 4 tenths on the top line. Clearly there are not enough so one of the 8 units on the top line is broken into extra tenths, leaving just 7 units in the units column and giving 14 tenths in the tenths column:

   9⁷8.⁴1 4
  -34.6

The child now subtracts the tenths, then the units, then the tens:

   9⁷8.⁴1 4
  -34.6
   63.8

Here are some questions that you could practise with your child. He/she will need to work in a book or on a separate piece of paper and will need to lay each question out in columns, making sure that the numbers are in the correct columns. Tidiness helps to avoid mistakes. Notice that in some of the questions there is no need to get extra tenths from one of the units because there are already enough tenths. In some questions your child will need to get extra units by using one of the tens.

(clue: write the 48 as 48.0)

① 36.7 - 12.9   ② 48 - 19.4   ③ 52.6 - 23.1   ④ 6.2 - 1.8

⑤ 18.7 - 9.9   ⑥ 84.3 - 37.8   ⑦ 15 - 7.5   ⑧ 67.4 - 48.7

If you find that your child is confident with these questions, try questions with hundredths as well as tenths. The process is the same: extra hundredths can be made by using one of the tenths, extra tenths can be made by using one of the units, extra units can be made by using one of the tens.

You may like to let us know how your child gets on with these activities – if so please return this sheet with any comments on the back.

Efficient written methods for subtraction of decimals

Worksheet 1

Name: _____

Date: _____

On this page I will be subtracting integers and decimals. The word 'integer' simply means 'whole number'.

Look at this example. 29.4 - 12.7

Step 1: Write the question out very neatly in columns.

$$\begin{array}{r} 29.4 \\ -17.7 \\ \hline \end{array}$$

Step 2: Look at the tenths first. We need to do 4 tenths subtract 7 tenths, but 4 is not enough to subtract 7 so we use one of the 9 units to make 10 extra tenths.

$$\begin{array}{r} 2\overset{8}{\cancel{9}}.^{1}4 \\ -17.7 \\ \hline \end{array}$$

Step 3: Now we can do 14 tenths subtract 7 tenths, which gives us 7 to put in the tenths part of the answer.

$$\begin{array}{r} 2\overset{8}{\cancel{9}}.^{1}4 \\ -17.7 \\ \hline .7 \end{array}$$

Step 4: Now we have 8 units to subtract 2 units. We have got enough units to do this and we have got enough tens to do the tens part of the question as well.

$$\begin{array}{r} 2\overset{8}{\cancel{9}}.^{1}4 \\ -17.7 \\ \hline 11.7 \end{array}$$

Use this method to answer the questions below. You will need to work neatly in your maths book or on a separate piece of paper. Remember to always check whether you need extra tenths or extra units. Sometimes you will have enough.

1 16.4 - 8.3   **2** 37.2 - 12.6   **3** 43.9 - 27.4

4 68.1 - 37.5   **5** 76.2 - 47.8   **6** 80 - 23.5

7 93.5 - 46.5   **8** 81.6 - 53.4   **9** 78.2 - 56.4

10 90 - 36.9   **11** 85.5 - 48.7   **12** 100 - 13.8

Efficient written methods for subtraction of decimals

Worksheet 2

Name: _____

Date: _____

Find the subtractions from 1.
You may be able to work these out in your head or you may need to do some calculations in your book or on a separate piece of paper.

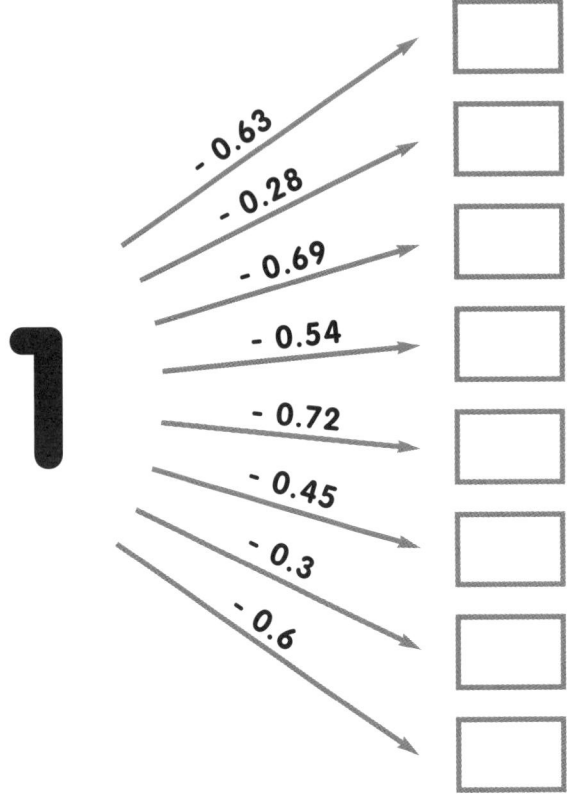

Now complete the following subtractions in your maths book. Work very neatly as you are less likely to make mistakes. Remember to write the numbers in the correct columns.

Here is the first question: 13 - 2.75
To work this out in the column method you will need to write it out like this:

```
  13.00
-  2.75
```

1. 13 - 2.75
2. 4.7 - 2.99
3. 6.89 - 1.45
4. 5.42 - 2.86
5. 12.49 - 5.73
6. 28.6 - 15.35
7. 8 - 1.84
8. 9.01 - 3.59
9. 10 - 2.65
10. 8.69 - 3.9
11. 15 - 6.04
12. 17.9 - 5.86

I can...
I can subtract integers and decimals. ☐
I know what the word 'integer' means. ☐

Factors and prime numbers

Teacher's notes

Building on previous learning
The ability to identify pairs of factors of two-digit whole numbers is a learning objective for Year 5 but revising it here gives practice in recalling multiplication facts as well as revealing the prime numbers. Before starting this unit check that the children can already:
- Recall multiplication facts up to 10 x 10 and the corresponding division facts.

Learning objectives
- Identify pairs of factors of two-digit whole numbers.
- Recognise that prime numbers have only two factors.

Learning outcomes
- The children will be able to identify all the factors of specified two-digit whole numbers.
- The children will observe that prime numbers have only two factors.
- The children will be able to find all prime numbers less than 100.

Success criteria
Can the children…
… find the factors of 16, 24, 36, 50, 81, 100?
… identify 13, 17, 23 and 37 as prime numbers and explain why?

Resources needed
- A display of multiplication tables to which the pupils can make reference but which can also be covered at the teacher's discretion when the pupils are confident enough to complete the multiplication grid without support.
- Multiplication grids and mixed multiplication grids for practice of tables facts.

Opportunities for using and applying the skills
- Solving multi-step problems, and problems involving fractions, decimals and percentages.
- Represent and interpret sequences, patterns and relationships involving numbers. Constant practice of multiplication tables can be frustrating for pupils but many pupils enjoy the opportunity to use their tables in investigations. An extension of the activities in this unit would be to find the prime factors of any two-digit number, which is a further learning objective for Year 6 e.g. you could ask the children to find the prime factors of 36. There are several ways to factorise 36, e.g. 6 x 6, 4 x 9, 3 x 12, 2 x 18. If the child picks any of these he/she can then take the next step of factorising the factors. So, for example, if 36 is factorised to 3 x 12, the 3 cannot be factorised because it is a prime number but the 12 could be factorised to 2 x 6 (other ways are possible). The 2 is a prime number so now the 6 can be factorised to 2 x 3. Nothing else can be done so we have found the prime factors: 3, 2, 2, 3. This process can be completed using a factor tree as shown, where the prime factors are circled. Encourage the children to notice that if the prime factors are multiplied together the product is 36:

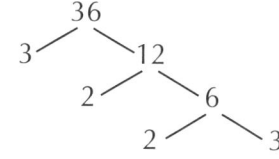

Factors and prime numbers
Help at home sheet

Child's name: **Date:**

Dear Parents

At school we follow the National Curriculum and the Primary Framework for mathematics. One aspect of our work in mathematics is the learning of number skills and part of that concerns finding factors and identifying prime numbers. The children have practised the multiplication tables from the two times-table to the ten times-table and we are now trying to strengthen that knowledge through further practice – the process of finding factors gives an excellent opportunity to practise tables. We are keen to involve parents in their children's learning so you may like to help your child by using some of the ideas on this sheet.

National Curriculum

The Primary Framework for mathematics says that Year 6 pupils should:
- recognise that prime numbers have only two factors.

You could...

... give your child a random two-digit number and ask him/her to find the factors. A good way to do this is to ask your child to write the number at the top of a list of factor pairs, like this:

<u>12</u>
1 x 12
12 x 1
2 x 6
6 x 2
3 x 4
4 x 3

Your child will need to use multiplication tables to find out the factors, especially with larger numbers.

You could choose some numbers that only have themselves and 1 as factors, e.g. 17:

<u>17</u>
1 x 17
17 x 1

Explain to your child that numbers like these are called prime numbers.

Keep practising with lots of numbers so that your child becomes confident in using mathematical vocabulary such as 'factor' and 'prime number'.

You may like to let us know how your child gets on with these activities – if so please return this sheet with any comments on the back.

Andrew Brodie: Number Journey for ages 10-11 © A&C Black Publishers Ltd 2008

Factors and prime numbers

Worksheet 1

Name: _____

Date: _____

On this page I will be finding pairs of factors.

Look at this number:

12

We can make 12 in several ways by multiplying integers (whole numbers) together:

```
      12
 1 x 12
12 x  1
 2 x  6
 6 x  2
 3 x  4
 4 x  3
```

The integers that can be multiplied to make 12 are called the factors of 12, so you can see that the factors of 12 are: 1, 2, 3, 4, 6, 12.

For each of the numbers below show the pairs of integers that can be multiplied together to make the number, then write a list of the factors of the number.

16
_____
_____
_____
_____

The factors of 16 are:
_____

24
_____
_____
_____
_____
_____
_____
_____

The factors of 24 are:
_____

36
_____
_____
_____
_____
_____

The factors of 36 are:
_____

100
_____
_____
_____
_____
_____
_____

50
_____
_____
_____
_____
_____

81
_____
_____
_____

The factors of 100 are:
_____

The factors of 50 are:
_____

The factors of 81 are:
_____

Factors and prime numbers

Worksheet 2

Name: _____

Date: _____

For each of the numbers below show the pairs of integers that can be multiplied together to make the number, then write a list of the factors of the number.

48

_____
_____
_____
_____
_____
_____
_____
_____

The factors of 48 are:

_____

60

_____
_____
_____
_____
_____
_____
_____
_____
_____
_____

The factors of 60 are:

_____

13

_____
_____

The factors of 13 are:

_____

17

_____
_____

The factors of 17 are:

_____

23

_____
_____

The factors of 23 are:

_____

37

_____
_____

The factors of 37 are:

_____

What do you notice about 13, 17, 23 and 37? Each of these numbers only has two factors – itself and 1. These numbers are called prime numbers.

There is only one even number that is a prime number. Do you know what it is?

_____

I can...
I can remember what factors are. ☐
I can remember what integers are. ☐
I can remember what prime numbers are. ☐

Square numbers and prime numbers

Teacher's notes

Building on previous learning
Before starting this unit check that the children can already:
- recall multiplication facts up to 10 x 10 and the corresponding division facts.
- identify pairs of factors of two-digit whole numbers.
- identify and explain prime numbers.

Learning objectives
- Identify pairs of factors of two-digit whole numbers.
- Recognise that prime numbers have only two factors.
- Identify prime numbers less than 100.
- Derive quickly squares of numbers to 12 x 12.

Learning outcomes
- The children will be able to find all square numbers to 12 x 12.
- The children will be familiar with the vocabulary and notation related to square numbers.
- The children will be able to find all prime numbers less than 100.

Success criteria
Can the children…
… find the answers to questions such as 4^2, 9^2, 2^2, 7^2, 5^2, 12^2?
… find all the prime numbers less than 100?

Resources needed
- A display of multiplication tables to which the pupils can make reference but which can also be covered at your discretion when the pupils are confident enough to complete the multiplication grid without support.
- Multiplication grids and mixed multiplication grids for practice of tables facts.

Opportunities for using and applying the skills
- Solving multi-step problems, and problems involving fractions, decimals and percentages.
- Choosing and using appropriate calculation strategies at each stage, including calculator use.
- This book is concerned with calculation strategies based on mental work and written work. Calculators are not required for any of the activities in the book.
- Represent and interpret sequences, patterns and relationships involving numbers. When finding pairs of factors do the pupils notice that the square numbers have an odd number of factor pairs whereas all other numbers have an even number of factor pairs? This is simply because one factor pair consists of the square root of the number multiplied by itself and therefore it would be the same if it was reversed:

$$\underline{16}$$
$$1 \times 16$$
$$16 \times 1$$
$$2 \times 8$$
$$8 \times 2$$
$$4 \times 4$$

Square numbers and prime numbers

Help at home sheet

Child's name: Date:

Dear Parents

At school we follow the National Curriculum and the Primary Framework for mathematics. One aspect of our work in mathematics is the learning of number skills and part of that concerns both identifying prime numbers and finding square numbers. The children have learnt how to identify prime numbers and, in school, will now be finding all the prime numbers less than 100. We will also be working on square numbers. We are keen to involve parents in their children's learning so you may like to help your child by using some of the ideas on this sheet.

National Curriculum

The Primary Framework for mathematics says that Year 6 pupils should:
- recognise that prime numbers have only two factors and identify prime numbers less than 100;
- use knowledge of multiplication facts to derive quickly squares of numbers to 12 x 12 and the corresponding squares of multiples of 10.

You could...

... ask your child to answer these questions, which they will find easy if they know their multiplication tables:

   2 x 2

   3 x 3

   4 x 4

   etc

Explain that the answers to these questions are called square numbers and that sometimes instead of saying 'two times two' or 'three times three' we might say 'two squared' or 'three squared', etc. Practise with your child giving random questions such as 'six squared', 'nine squared', 'ten squared', etc.

Some children find this question difficult: 1 x 1. Most of the multiplications that they have ever done have resulted in answers that are bigger than the two numbers being multiplied together but this one is very unusual in that the answer is 1. '1 x 1 = 1' or 'one squared is one'.

In most of our multiplication practice we have learnt the tables as far as 10 x but some people like to go on to 11 x and 12 x. You could practise the tables to 12 x with your child, then ask him/her to tell you what eleven squared is and what twelve squared is. Keep practising so that your child becomes confident in using mathematical vocabulary such as 'square number' or 'eight squared', etc.

You may like to let us know how your child gets on with these activities – if so please return this sheet with any comments on the back.

Andrew Brodie: Number Journey for ages 10-11 © A&C Black Publishers Ltd 2008

Square numbers and prime numbers

Worksheet 1

Name: _____

Date: _____

On this page I will be finding square numbers.

Write the answers to these questions:

2 x 2 = ☐   6 x 6 = ☐   9 x 9 = ☐   10 x 10 = ☐

The answers you have written are called square numbers.

Look:

• • • •
• • • •   This shows 4 x 4 = 16.
• • • •
• • • •

Here are some things we could say about it.

- Four squared is sixteen.
- The square of four is sixteen.
- Sixteen is a square number.
- The square root of sixteen is four.

Answer the following questions.

What is five squared? ☐   What is the square of three? ☐

What is the square of seven? ☐   How much is eleven squared? ☐

How much is eight squared? ☐   What is twelve squared? ☐

What is one squared? ☐

(Be careful with this one - you may be surprised by the answer.)

Now look at a quick way of writing 3 x 3 = 9 ⟶ $3^2 = 9$

Write the answers to the following questions.

4^2 = ☐ 9^2 = ☐ 2^2 = ☐ 7^2 = ☐ 5^2 = ☐ 12^2 = ☐

Andrew Brodie: Number Journey for ages 10-11 © A&C Black Publishers Ltd 2008

Square numbers and prime numbers

Worksheet 2

Name: _____

Date: _____

Use the grid below to find all the prime numbers less than 100.

1. Cross out the number 1 as it is not prime because it has only one factor.
2. Leave 2 as it is a prime number but cross out every multiple of 2 (4, 6, 8, ...)
3. Leave 3 as it is a prime number but cross out every multiple of 3 (6, 9, 12, ...)
4. Leave 5 as it is a prime number but cross out every multiple of 5 (10, 15, 20, ...)
5. Leave 7 as it is a prime number but cross out every multiple of 7 (14, 21, 28, ...)

1	2	3	4	5	6	7	8	9	10
11	12	13	14	15	16	17	18	19	20
21	22	23	24	25	26	27	28	29	30
31	32	33	34	35	36	37	38	39	40
41	42	43	44	45	46	47	48	49	50
51	52	53	54	55	56	57	58	59	60
61	62	63	64	65	66	67	68	69	70
71	72	73	74	75	76	77	78	79	80
81	82	83	84	85	86	87	88	89	90
91	92	93	94	95	96	97	98	99	100

The numbers that are left uncrossed are all prime numbers.

List all the prime numbers between 1 and 100:

☐ ☐ ☐ ☐ ☐ ☐ ☐ ☐ ☐ ☐
☐ ☐ ☐ ☐ ☐ ☐ ☐ ☐ ☐ ☐
☐ ☐ ☐ ☐ ☐

I can...
- I can remember what factors are. ☐
- I can remember what integers are. ☐
- I know what prime numbers are. ☐
- I know what square numbers are. ☐

Using multiplication facts to 10 x 10 to derive related multiplication facts involving decimals

Teacher's notes

Building on previous learning
Before starting this unit check that the children can already:
- recall multiplication facts up to 10 x 10.
- explain what each digit represents in whole numbers and decimals with up to two places, and partition, round and order these numbers.

Learning objectives
- Recall multiplication facts up to 10 x 10.
- Use the multiplication facts to derive related multiplication facts involving decimals.

Learning outcomes
The children will be able to:
- recall multiplication facts up to 10 x 10.
- use the multiplication facts to find multiplication facts involving decimals.
- identify and use patterns, relationships and properties of numbers.

Success criteria
Can the children…
… recall the multiplication facts to 10 x 10?
… use the multiplication facts to find facts involving multiplying decimals such as:
0.2, 0.7, 0.4, 0.9, 0.3, 0.8, 0.5, 0.6?

Resources needed
- A display of multiplication tables to which the pupils can make reference but which can also be covered at the teacher's discretion when the pupils are confident enough.

Opportunities for using and applying the skills
- Solving multi-step problems, and problems involving fractions, decimals and percentages.
- Choosing and using appropriate calculation strategies at each stage, including calculator use. This book is concerned with calculation strategies based on mental work and written work. Calculators are not required for any of the activities in the book.
- Represent and interpret sequences, patterns and relationships involving numbers: Pupils will use their knowledge of place value to be able to multiply decimals with one place by integers.

Andrew Brodie: Number Journey for ages 10-11 © A&C Black Publishers Ltd 2008

Using multiplication facts to 10 × 10 to derive related multiplication facts involving decimals

Help at home sheet

Child's name: **Date:**

Dear Parents
At school we follow the National Curriculum and the Primary Framework for mathematics. One aspect of our work in mathematics is the learning of number skills and part of that concerns practising all the multiplication tables. The children have practised the multiplication tables from the two times-table to the ten times-table and we are now seeking to strengthen that knowledge through further practice by using the tables to find multiplication facts involving decimals. We are keen to involve parents in their children's learning so you may like to help your child by using some of the ideas on this sheet.

National Curriculum

The Primary Framework for Mathematics says that Year 6 pupils should:
- Use knowledge of place value and multiplication facts to 10 × 10 to derive related multiplication and division facts involving decimals.

You could...

… draw some sketches of 'decimal cakes' like these:

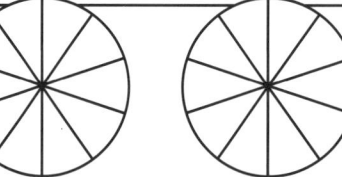

Now ask your child to find the answer to this question: 6 × 0.3

- Encourage him/her to colour in 0.3 on the first cake, then another 0.3 on that cake, and another 0.3 on that cake.
- That's three lots of 0.3 so far but now only 0.1 can be coloured on the first cake and 0.2 will need to be coloured on the second cake.
- Now your child can colour 0.3 on that cake and another 0.3 on that cake.

- He/she has coloured six lots of 0.3 – ask how much has been coloured altogether and he/she should come up with the answer 'one point eight'.
- Write the question and answer down: 6 × 0.3 = 1.8 Your child may see the link to the times tables: 6 × 3 = 18 so 6 × 0.3 = 1.8

If further practice is needed draw more decimal cakes and try questions such as 4 × 0.5, 7 × 0.2, 5 × 0.3

Once your child is confident, try timing each of the columns of questions in this grid.

7 × 0.4 =	2 × 0.9 =	6 × 0.2 =
9 × 0.5 =	4 × 0.6 =	4 × 0.9 =
2 × 0.4 =	9 × 0.3 =	8 × 0.3 =
5 × 0.6 =	6 × 0.7 =	5 × 0.5 =
7 × 0.9 =	8 × 0.4 =	7 × 0.8 =
6 × 0.8 =	10 × 0.9 =	10 × 0.6 =

You may like to let us know how your child gets on with these activities – if so please return this sheet with any comments on the back.

Using multiplication facts to 10 × 10 to derive related multiplication facts involving decimals

Worksheet 1

Name: _____

Date: _____

On this page I will be using my multiplication tables to find answers to multiplications involving decimals.

Look:
- 6 × 5 = 30 … so 6 × 0.5 = 3
- 4 × 8 = 32 … so 4 × 0.8 = 3.2
- 3 × 9 = 27 … so 0.3 × 9 = 2.7
- 5 × 9 = 45 … so 0.5 × 9 = 4.5

Find the answers to the multiplications shown. How quickly can you complete each set?

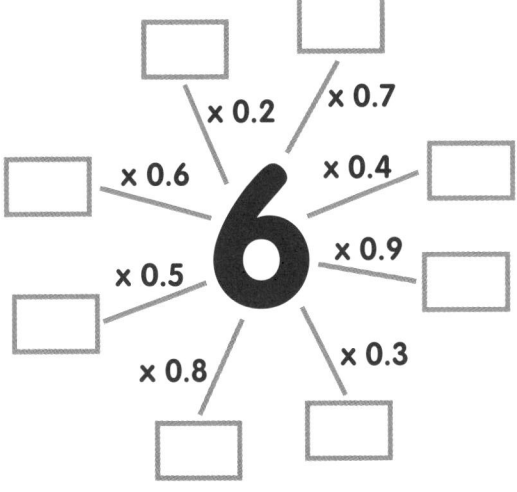
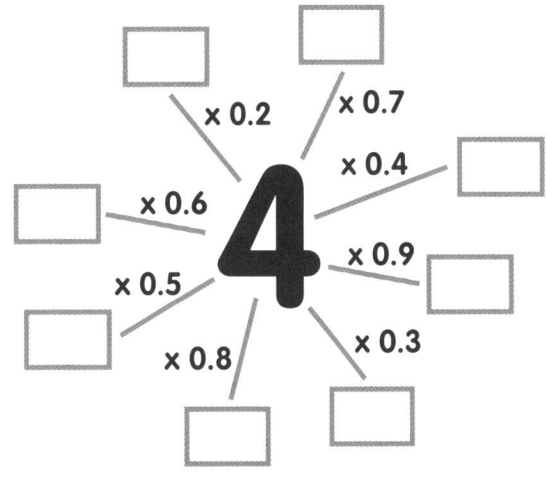
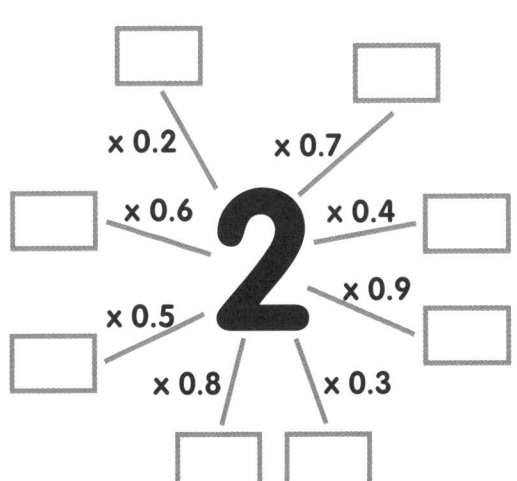
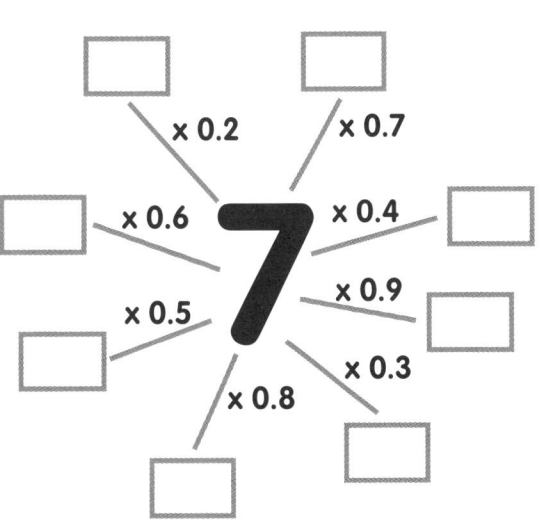

Andrew Brodie: Number Journey for ages 10-11 © A&C Black Publishers Ltd 2008

Using multiplication facts to 10 x 10 to derive related multiplication facts involving decimals

Worksheet 2

Name: _____

Date: _____

Find the answers to the multiplications shown.
How quickly can you complete each set?

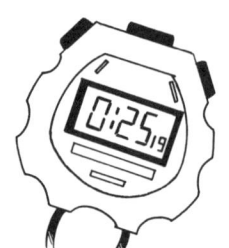

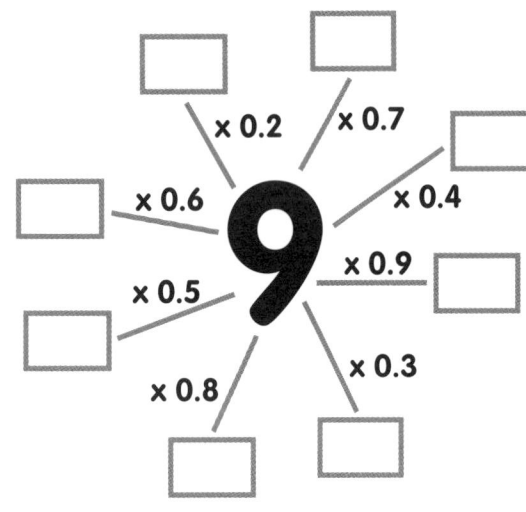

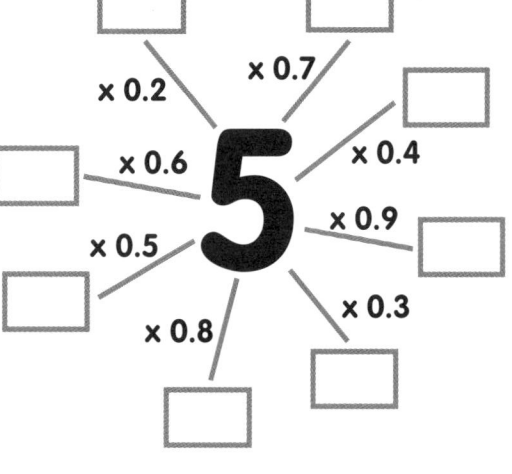

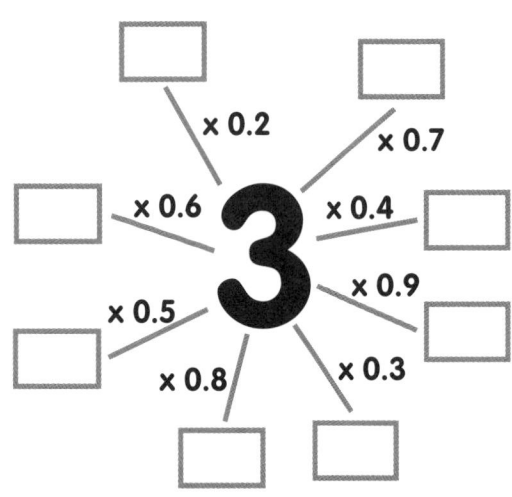

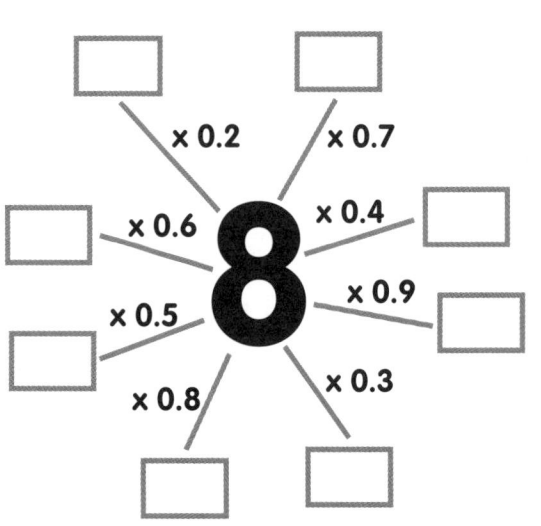

I can... I can remember my multiplication tables. ☐
I can use my multiplication tables to find multiplication facts involving decimals. ☐

Andrew Brodie: Number Journey for ages 10-11 © A&C Black Publishers Ltd 2008

Using multiplication facts to 10 x 10 to derive related division facts involving decimals

Teacher's notes

Building on previous learning
Before starting this unit check that the children can already:
- recall multiplication facts up to 10 x 10
- use the multiplication facts to find corresponding division facts
- explain what each digit represents in whole numbers and decimals with up to two places, and partition, round and order these numbers

Learning objectives
- Recall multiplication facts up to 10 x 10.
- Use the multiplication facts to derive related division facts involving decimals.

Learning outcomes
- The children will be able to recall multiplication facts up to 10 x 10.
- The children will be able to use the multiplication facts to find division facts involving decimals.
- The children will be able to identify and use patterns, relationships and properties of numbers.

Success criteria
Can the children…
… recall the multiplication facts to answer division questions such as:
4.8 ÷ 8, 4.8 ÷ 4, 4.8 ÷ 2, 4.8 ÷ 6, 4.8 ÷ 3?
… extend the multiplication facts to find answers to questions such as:
4.8 ÷ 24, 4.8 ÷ 12, 4.8 ÷ 16?
… derive all the division facts with one-place decimal or integer answers for numbers such as:
1.8, 2.4, 2.1, 1.6, 2.8, 3.6, 4, 4.8?

Resources needed
- A display of multiplication tables to which the pupils can make reference but which can also be covered at the teacher's discretion when the pupils are confident enough.

Opportunities for using and applying the skills
- Solving multi-step problems, and problems involving fractions, decimals and percentages.
- Choosing and using appropriate calculation strategies at each stage, including calculator use.
- This book is concerned with calculation strategies based on mental work and written work. Calculators are not required for any of the activities in the book.
- Represent and interpret sequences, patterns and relationships involving numbers: Pupils will use their knowledge of place value to be able to divide decimals with one place by integers where the answers are decimals to one place and to divide numbers with up to one decimal place by decimals with one place where the answers are integers.

Using multiplication facts to 10 x 10 to derive related division facts involving decimals

Help at home sheet

Child's name: Date:

Dear Parents

At school we follow the National Curriculum and the Primary Framework for mathematics. One aspect of our work in mathematics is the learning of number skills and part of that concerns practising all the multiplication tables. The children have practised the multiplication tables from the two times-table to the ten times-table and we are now seeking to strengthen that knowledge through further practice by using the tables to find division facts involving decimals. We are keen to involve parents in their children's learning so you may like to help your child by using some of the ideas on this sheet.

National Curriculum

The Primary Framework for Mathematics says that Year 6 pupils should:
- use knowledge of place value and multiplication facts to 10 x 10 to derive related multiplication and division facts involving decimals.

You could...

... draw some sketches of 'decimal cakes' like these:

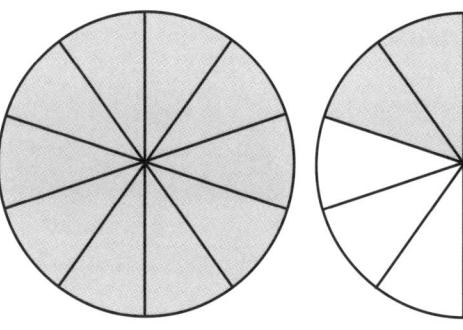

Now ask your child to find the answer to this question: 1.2 ÷ 4

Discuss how the 1.2 cakes could be shared out between four people – how many slices would they have each?

Encourage your child to realise that each slice is one tenth of a whole cake and that each person would have three slices.

Write the question and answer down: 1.2 ÷ 4 = 0.3

Your child may see the link to the times tables: 4 x 3 = 12 so 12 ÷ 4 = 3 so 1.2 ÷ 4 = 0.3

If further practice is needed, draw more decimal cakes and try questions such as 1.8 ÷ 6, 2.4 ÷ 3

Once your child is confident, try timing each of the columns of questions in this grid.

2.4 ÷ 6 =	1.2 ÷ 6 =	3.6 ÷ 6 =
1.2 ÷ 3 =	1.6 ÷ 4 =	4.2 ÷ 7 =
1.5 ÷ 5 =	3.6 ÷ 9 =	3.2 ÷ 4 =
2.1 ÷ 3 =	4.8 ÷ 6 =	1.5 ÷ 3 =
2.5 ÷ 5 =	3.2 ÷ 8 =	2.8 ÷ 4 =
2.8 ÷ 7 =	1.8 ÷ 9 =	3 ÷ 6 =

You may like to let us know how your child gets on with these activities – if so please return this sheet with any comments on the back.

Andrew Brodie: Number Journey for ages 10-11 © A&C Black Publishers Ltd 2008

Using multiplication facts to 10 x 10 to derive related division facts involving decimals

Worksheet 1

Name: _____

Date: _____

On this page I will be using my multiplication tables to find answers to divisions involving decimals.

Look: 6 x 5 = 30   ... so 30 ÷ 6 = 5   so 3 ÷ 6 = 0.5

4 x 8 = 32   ... so 32 ÷ 4 = 8   so 3.2 ÷ 4 = 0.8

3 x 9 = 27   ... so 27 ÷ 9 = 3   so 2.7 ÷ 9 = 0.3

5 x 9 = 45   ... so 45 ÷ 5 = 9   so 4.5 ÷ 5 = 0.9

Find the answers to the divisions shown.
How quickly can you complete each set?

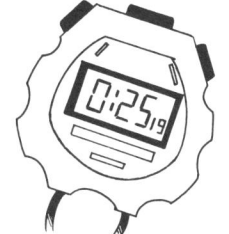

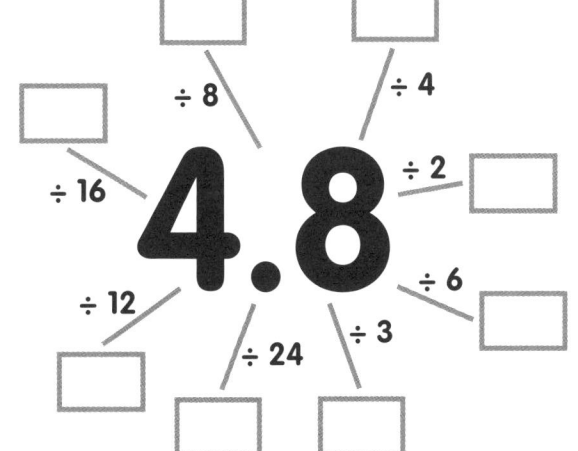

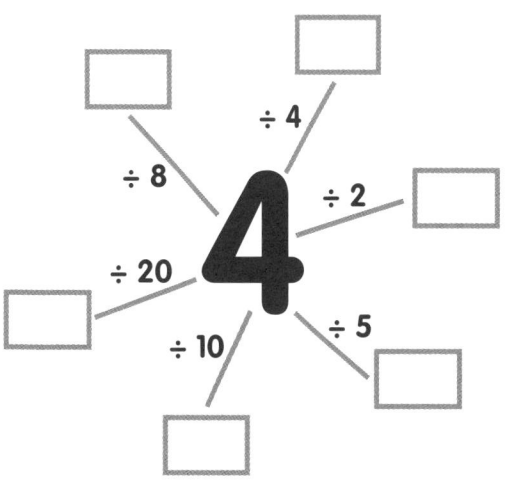

35

Using multiplication facts to 10 x 10 to derive related division facts involving decimals

Worksheet 2

Name: _____

Date: _____

For each number below, show the division facts that can be found where the answer is either a decimal with one place or an integer. The first one has been done for you.

3.2

3.2 ÷ 4 = 0.8
3.2 ÷ 8 = 0.4
3.2 ÷ 2 = 1.6
3.2 ÷ 16 = 0.2
3.2 ÷ 0.8 = 4
3.2 ÷ 0.4 = 8
3.2 ÷ 0.2 = 16
3.2 ÷ 1.6 = 2

1.8

2.4

2.1

4.8

3.6

4

1.6

2.8

I can...
I can remember my multiplication tables. ☐
I can use my multiplication tables to find division facts involving decimals. ☐

Using efficient written methods for the multiplication of a two-digit or three-digit number by a one-digit number

Teacher's notes

Building on previous learning
Pupils will already have multiplied two-digit and three-digit numbers by one-digit numbers in previous school years but may well have used a grid method. The method used in this unit is the compact method of short multiplication. Some schools may prefer to use an expanded form of short multiplication before this method. Every school needs a clear written policy on calculation methods and when to use them. Before starting this unit check that the children can already:
- use practical and informal written methods to multiply two-digit numbers.
- use written methods to record, support and explain multiplication of two-digit numbers by a one-digit number.
- recall quickly multiplication facts up to 10 x 10.
- partition three-digit numbers into multiples of 100, 10 and 1.
- add two-digit and three-digit whole numbers quickly and efficiently.

Learning objectives
- Use efficient written methods for the multiplication of two-digit and three-digit numbers by one-digit numbers.

Learning outcomes
- The children will be able to multiply two-digit numbers by one-digit numbers using the compact form of short multiplication.
- The children will be able to multiply three-digit numbers by one-digit numbers using the compact form of short multiplication.

Success criteria
Can the children…
… use the short multiplication method to answer these questions:
48 x 4, 36 x 7, 65 x 9, 63 x 8, 72 x 4, 87 x 6, 53 x 9, 98 x 3, 75 x 5, 25 x 9, 38 x 7, 91 x 5?
… use the short multiplication method to answer these questions:
365 x 4, 219 x 6, 182 x 4, 206 x 7, 528 x 3, 618 x 5, 147 x 9, 802 x 4, 789 x 8, 592 x 2, 846 x 3, 999 x 9?

Resources needed
- A clear school policy on the systems and methods to be used in recording multiplications both informally and formally.
- A display of multiplication tables.
- Multiplication grids for pupils who are not able to recall multiplication facts quickly.

Opportunities for using and applying the skills
- Solving multi-step problems, and problems involving fractions, decimals and percentages.
- Choosing and using appropriate calculation strategies at each stage, including calculator use. This book is concerned with calculation strategies based on mental work and written work. Calculators are not required for any of the activities in the book.
- Represent and interpret sequences, patterns and relationships involving numbers: pupils will use their understanding of place value to multiply and 'carry' digits.

Using efficient written methods for the multiplication of a two-digit or three-digit number by a one-digit number

Help at home sheet

Child's name: Date:

Dear Parents

At school we follow the National Curriculum and the Primary Framework for mathematics. One aspect of our work in mathematics is the learning of number skills, including using written methods for the multiplication of three-digit numbers by one-digit numbers. There are lots of methods that can be used for multiplication, including a very effective method using a grid. The method that we are showing on this sheet is the 'traditional' short form of multiplication. We are keen to involve parents in their children's learning so you may like to help your child by using some of the ideas on this sheet.

National Curriculum

The Primary Framework for Mathematics says that Year 6 pupils should:
- use efficient written methods to multiply and divide integers and decimals by a one-digit integer.

You could...

... practise multiplications with your child using the method outlined here.

To find the answer to a multiplication question such as 257 x 3 we write it out like this:

$$\begin{array}{r} 257 \\ \times\ 3 \\ \hline \end{array}$$

Step 1: Multiply the units: 7 x 3 = 21 Because the number 21 is made up of 2 tens and 1 unit, the 1 is written in the units column and the 2 is written as small as possible below the tens column:

$$\begin{array}{r} 257 \\ \times\ 3 \\ \hline {}_21 \end{array}$$

Step 2: Multiply the tens: 5 tens x 3 = 15 tens. Now add the 2 tens that were 'carried' from the units to make a total of 17 tens. Because 17 tens is worth 10 tens and 7 tens, the 7 is written in the tens column and a very small 1 is written below the hundreds column.

$$\begin{array}{r} 257 \\ \times\ 3 \\ \hline {}_1 7{}_2 1 \end{array}$$

Step 3: Multiply the hundreds: 2 hundreds x 3 = 6 hundreds. Now add the 1 hundred that was 'carried' from the tens to give a total of 7 hundreds – the 7 can be written in the hundreds column. Note that sometimes there will be 10 or more hundreds and therefore a number may need to be written in the thousands column.

$$\begin{array}{r} 257 \\ \times\ 3 \\ \hline 77{}_1 {}_2 1 \end{array}$$

Ask your child to use this method to answer the following questions. Make sure that he/she works neatly in an exercise book or on paper and that he/she follows the method shown in the example.

1. 294 x 3
2. 368 x 4
3. 519 x 7
4. 847 x 2
5. 963 x 9

You may like to let us know how your child gets on with these activities – if so please return this sheet with any comments on the back.

Using efficient written methods for the multiplication of a two-digit or three-digit number by a one-digit number

Worksheet 1

Name: _____

Date: _____

On this page I am going to multiply a two-digit number by a one-digit number.

To find the answer to a multiplication question such as 79 × 3 we write it out like this:

$$\begin{array}{r} 79 \\ \times 3 \\ \hline \end{array}$$

Step 1: Multiply the units: 9 × 3 = 27
Because the number 27 is made up of 2 tens and 7 units, the 7 is written in the units column and the 2 is written as small as possible below the tens column:

$$\begin{array}{r} 79 \\ \times 3 \\ \hline _{2}7 \end{array}$$

Step 2: Multiply the tens: 7 tens × 3 = 21 tens. Now add the 2 tens that were 'carried' from the units to make a total of 23 tens. 23 tens is worth 20 tens and 3 tens, so the 3 is written in the tens column and the 2 is written in the hundreds column because 20 tens are worth 2 hundreds.

$$\begin{array}{r} 79 \\ \times 3 \\ \hline 23_{2}7 \end{array}$$

Here are some questions that you can complete in your exercise book or on a separate sheet of paper. Work very neatly using the method shown on this sheet.

1. 48 × 4
2. 36 × 7
3. 65 × 9
4. 63 × 8
5. 72 × 4
6. 87 × 6
7. 53 × 9
8. 98 × 3
9. 75 × 5
10. 25 × 9
11. 38 × 7
12. 91 × 5

Andrew Brodie: Number Journey for ages 10-11 © A&C Black Publishers Ltd 2008

Using efficient written methods for the multiplication of a two-digit or three-digit number by a one-digit number

Worksheet 2

Name: _____

Date: _____

To find the answer to a multiplication question such as 472 × 3 we write it out like this:

```
  472
×   3
```

Step 1: Multiply the units: 2 × 3 = 6
Because the answer is less than 10, the 6 is written in the units column and there is no need to 'carry' a number to the tens column:

```
  472
×   3
    6
```

Step 2: Multiply the tens: 7 tens × 3 = 21 tens. 21 tens is worth 20 tens and 1 ten, so the 1 is written in the tens column and the 2 is written as small as possible in the hundreds column because 20 tens are worth 2 hundreds.

```
  472
×   3
  ₂16
```

Step 3: Multiply the hundreds: 4 hundreds × 3 = 12 hundreds. Add the two hundreds that were carried from the tens to give a total of 14 hundreds ~ the 4 can be written in the hundreds column and the 1 is written in the thousands column.

```
  472
×   3
 14₂16
```

Here are some questions that you can complete in your exercise book or on a separate sheet of paper. Work very neatly using the method shown on this sheet.

1. 365 × 4
2. 219 × 6
3. 182 × 4
4. 206 × 7
5. 528 × 3
6. 618 × 5
7. 147 × 9
8. 802 × 4
9. 789 × 8
10. 592 × 2
11. 846 × 3
12. 999 × 9

I can... I can multiply three-digit numbers by one-digit numbers using short multiplication. ☐

Using efficient written methods for the multiplication of integers and decimals by a one-digit number

Teacher's notes

Building on previous learning
Pupils will already have multiplied two-digit and three-digit numbers by one-digit numbers in previous school years but may well have used a grid method. The method used in this unit is the compact method of short multiplication. Some schools may prefer to use an expanded form of short multiplication before this method. Each school needs a clear written policy on calculation methods and when to use them. Before starting this unit check that the children can already:
- use practical and informal written methods to multiply two-digit numbers
- use written methods to record, support and explain multiplication of two-digit numbers by a one-digit number
- recall quickly multiplication facts up to 10 x 10
- partition integers and decimals into multiples of 100, 10, 1, $\frac{1}{10}$ and $\frac{1}{100}$

Learning objectives
- Use efficient written methods for the multiplication of integers and decimals by one-digit numbers.

Learning outcomes
- The children will be able to multiply integers and decimals to one place by a one-digit number.
- The children will be able to multiply integers and decimals to two places by a one-digit number.

Success criteria
Can the children…
… multiply numbers containing decimals with one place by one-digit numbers:
1.9 x 4, 2.8 x 6, 3.7 x 9, 5.4 x 8, 6.7 x 4, 3.9 x 6, 8.1 x 9, 12.4 x 3, 13.7 x 5, 24.6 x 7, 38.4 x 3, 62.9 x 2?
… multiply numbers containing decimals with two places by one-digit numbers:
1.65 x 4, 2.32 x 6, 6.45 x 4, 7.19 x 7, 4.63 x 3, 6.08 x 5, 5.07 x 9, 6.29 x 4, 12.25 x 8, 16.43 x 2, 28.75 x 3, 42.25 x 9?

Resources needed
- A clear school policy on the systems and methods to be used in recording multiplications both informally and formally.
- A display of multiplication tables.
- Multiplication grids for pupils who are not able to recall multiplication facts quickly.

Opportunities for using and applying the skills
- Solving multi-step problems, and problems involving fractions, decimals and percentages.
- Choosing and using appropriate calculation strategies at each stage, including calculator use. This book is concerned with calculation strategies based on mental work and written work. Calculators are not required for any of the activities in the book.
- Represent and interpret sequences, patterns and relationships involving numbers: pupils will use their understanding of place value to multiply and 'carry' digits, including those involved in decimals up to two places.

Using efficient written methods for the multiplication of integers and decimals by a one-digit number

Help at home sheet

Child's name: Date:

Dear Parents

At school we follow the National Curriculum and the Primary Framework for mathematics. One aspect of our work in mathematics is the learning of number skills, including using written methods for the multiplication of whole numbers and decimals by one-digit numbers. We are keen to involve parents in their children's learning so you may like to help your child by using some of the ideas on this sheet.

National Curriculum

The Primary Framework for Mathematics says that Year 6 pupils should:
- use efficient written methods to multiply and divide integers and decimals by a one-digit integer.

You could...

... practise multiplications with your child using the method outlined here.

To find the answer to a multiplication question such as 2.6 x 3 we write it out like this:

$$\begin{array}{r} 2.6 \\ \times 3 \\ \hline \end{array}$$

Note that the 3 is written in the units column not the tenths column.

Step 1: Multiply the tenths: 6 tenths x 3 = 18 tenths
18 tenths is worth the same as 1 unit and 8 tenths so the 8 is written in the tenths column and the 1 is 'carried' to the units column:

$$\begin{array}{r} 2.6 \\ \times 3 \\ \hline {}_1.8 \end{array}$$

Note that the decimal point has been written on the answer line.

Step 2: Multiply the units: 2 units x 3 = 6.
Now add the 1 unit that was carried from the tenths to give a total of 7 units.

$$\begin{array}{r} 2.6 \\ \times 3 \\ \hline 7_1.8 \end{array}$$

Ask your child to use this method to answer the following questions. Make sure that he/she works neatly in an exercise book or on paper and that he/she follows the method shown in the example.

1 1.9 x 2   **2** 2.4 x 4   **3** 3.7 x 5   **4** 8.6 x 7   **5** 9.3 x 8

You may like to let us know how your child gets on with these activities – if so please return this sheet with any comments on the back.

Using efficient written methods for the multiplication of integers and decimals by a one-digit number

Worksheet 1

Name: _____

Date: _____

On this page I am going to multiply a number that includes a decimal to one place by a one-digit number.

To find the answer to a multiplication question such as 5.7 x 3 we write it out like this:

$$\begin{array}{r} 5.7 \\ \times\ 3 \\ \hline \end{array}$$

Note that the 3 is written in the units column not the tenths column.

Step 1: Multiply the tenths.
7 tenths x 3 = 21 tenths
21 tenths is worth the same as 2 units and 1 tenth so the 1 is written in the tenths column and the 2 is 'carried' to the units column:

$$\begin{array}{r} 5.7 \\ \times\ 3 \\ \hline _2.1 \end{array}$$

Note that the decimal point has been written on the answer line.

Step 2: Multiply the units: 5 units x 3 = 15 units. Now add the 2 units that were carried from the tenths to give a total of 17 units. 17 units are worth the same as 1 ten and 7 units so we write the 7 in the units column and the 1 in the tens column.

$$\begin{array}{r} 5.7 \\ \times\ 3 \\ \hline 17_2.1 \end{array}$$

Here are some questions that you can complete in your exercise book or on a separate piece of paper. Work very neatly using the method shown on this sheet.

1. 1.9 x 4
2. 2.8 x 6
3. 3.7 x 9
4. 5.4 x 8
5. 6.7 x 4
6. 3.9 x 6
7. 8.1 x 9
8. 12.4 x 3
9. 13.7 x 5
10. 24.6 x 7
11. 38.4 x 3
12. 62.9 x 2

Using efficient written methods for the multiplication of integers and decimals by a one-digit number

Worksheet 2

Name: _____

Date: _____

To find the answer to a multiplication question such as 6.25 × 7 we write it out like this:

```
  6.25
×    7
_____
```

Note that the 7 is written in the units column not the tenths column or the hundredths column.

Step 1: Multiply the hundredths:
5 hundredths × 7 = 35 hundredths
35 hundredths is worth the same as 3 tenths and 5 hundredths so the 5 is written in the hundredths column and the 3 is 'carried' to the tenths column:

```
  6.25
×    7
_____
   .₃5
```

Note that the decimal point has been written on the answer line.

Step 2: Multiply the tenths: 2 tenths × 7 = 14 tenths. Now add the 3 tenths that were carried from the hundredths to give a total of 17 tenths. 17 tenths are worth the same as 1 unit and 7 tenths so we write the 7 in the tenths column and the 1 in the units column.

```
  6.25
×    7
_____
  ₁.₃75
```

Step 3: Multiply the units: 6 units × 7 = 42 units. Now add the 1 unit that was carried from the tenths to give a total of 43 units ~ 3 can be written in the units column and 4 can be written in the tens column.

```
  6.25
×    7
_____
 43.₁₃75
```

Here are some questions that you can complete in your exercise book or on a separate piece of paper. Work very neatly using the method shown on this sheet.

① 1.65 × 4   ② 2.32 × 6   ③ 6.45 × 4
④ 7.19 × 7   ⑤ 4.63 × 3   ⑥ 6.08 × 5
⑦ 5.07 × 9   ⑧ 6.29 × 4   ⑨ 12.25 × 8
⑩ 16.43 × 2   ⑪ 28.75 × 3   ⑫ 42.25 × 9

I can...
I can multiply numbers containing decimals with one place by one-digit numbers. ☐
I can multiply numbers containing decimals with two places by one-digit numbers. ☐

Using efficient written methods for the multiplication of two-digit integers by a two-digit integer

Teacher's notes

Building on previous learning
Pupils will already have multiplied two-digit and three-digit numbers by two-digit numbers in previous school years but may well have used a grid method. The method used in this unit is the compact method of long multiplication. Some schools may prefer to use an expanded form of long multiplication before this method. Every school needs a clear written policy on calculation methods and when to use them. Before starting this unit check that the children can already:
- use written methods to record, support and explain multiplication of two-digit numbers by a one-digit number.
- recall quickly multiplication facts up to 10 x 10.

Learning objectives
- Use efficient written methods for the multiplication of two-digit integers by a two-digit integer.

Learning outcomes
- The children will be able to multiply two-digit integers by a two-digit integer.
- The children will be able to calculate the squares of two-digit integers.

Success criteria
Can the children…
… multiply the following questions involving two-digit integers multiply two-digit integers:
46 x 23, 52 x 18, 73 x 35, 98 x 47, 82 x 27, 63 x 48, 94 x 42, 77 x 54?
… calculate the value of the following square numbers:
25^2, 18^2, 36^2, 27^2?

Resources needed
- A clear school policy on the systems and methods to be used in recording multiplications both informally and formally.
- A display of multiplication tables
- Multiplication grids for pupils who are not able to recall multiplication facts quickly.

Opportunities for using and applying the skills
- Solving multi-step problems, and problems involving fractions, decimals and percentages.
- Choosing and using appropriate calculation strategies at every stage, including calculator use. This book is concerned with calculation strategies based on mental work and written work. Calculators are not required for any of the activities in the book.
- Represent and interpret sequences, patterns and relationships involving numbers: pupils will use their understanding of place value to multiply and 'carry' digits.
- Pupils will be able to use their skill in multiplication of two-digit integers to be able to find the squares of two-digit integers.

Using efficient written methods for the multiplication of two-digit integers by a two-digit integer

Help at home sheet

Child's name: Date:

Dear Parents

At school we follow the National Curriculum and the Primary Framework for mathematics. One aspect of our work in mathematics is the learning of number skills, including using written methods for the multiplication of two-digit whole numbers by two-digit whole numbers. We are keen to involve parents in their children's learning so you may like to help your child by using some of the ideas on this sheet.

National Curriculum

The Primary Framework for mathematics says that Year 5 pupils should:
- use efficient written methods to multiply two-digit and three-digit integers by a two-digit integer.

You could...

... practise multiplications with your child using the method outlined here. Notice that we are multiplying by the tens first rather than by the units first - in this way the children are less likely to forget to write a zero in the units column. To find the answer to a multiplication question such as 36 x 24 we write it out like this:

```
   36
 x 24
```

Step 1: Multiply the 6 units by the 2 tens: 6 x 20 = 120. The 0 is written in the units column, the 2 is written in the tens column and the 1 is written as small as possible below the hundreds:

```
   36
 x 24
  ₁20
```

Step 2: Multiply the 3 tens by the 2 tens: 30 x 20 = 600. This gives 6 for the hundreds column, plus the 1 that was carried from the tens so 7 is written in the hundreds:

```
   36
 x 24
  7₁20
```

Steps 3 and 4: Multiply 36 by 4, by multiplying 6 x 4 = 24, then 30 x 4 = 120:

```
   36
 x 24
  7₁20
  14₂4
```

Step 5: Add the two answers together:

```
   36
 x 24
  7₁20
 +14₂4
   864
```

You may like to let us know how your child gets on with these activities – if so please return this sheet with any comments on the back.

Using efficient written methods for the multiplication of two-digit integers by a two-digit integer

Worksheet 1

Name: _____

Date: _____

On this page I am going to multiply a two-digit integer by another two-digit integer. Do you remember what an integer is? An integer is a whole number so, for example, 32 is an integer but 32.4 is not an integer.

To find the answer to a multiplication question such as 48 × 32 we write it out like this:

$$\begin{array}{r} 48 \\ \times\ 32 \\ \hline \end{array}$$

Step 1: Multiply the 8 units by the 3 tens: 8 × 30 = 240. The 0 is written in the units column, the 4 is written in the tens column and the 2 is written as small as possible below the hundreds:

$$\begin{array}{r} 48 \\ \times\ 32 \\ \hline 40 \\ {}_2\ \end{array}$$

Step 2: Multiply the 4 tens by the 3 tens: 40 × 30 = 1200. This gives 1 for the thousands column and 2 for the hundreds column, plus the 2 that was carried from the tens so 4 is written in the hundreds and 1 is written in the thousands:

$$\begin{array}{r} 48 \\ \times\ 32 \\ \hline 144_20 \end{array}$$

Step 3: multiply the 8 by the 2: 8 × 2 = 16 so 6 is written in the units, below the last answer, and the 1 is carried to the tens:

$$\begin{array}{r} 48 \\ \times\ 32 \\ \hline 144_20 \\ {}_16 \end{array}$$

Step 4: Multiply the 4 tens by the 2: 40 × 2 = 80 This gives us 8 for the tens column but we need to add the 1 that we carried from the units so we write 9 in the tens:

$$\begin{array}{r} 48 \\ \times\ 32 \\ \hline 144_20 \\ 9_16 \end{array}$$

Step 5: Add the answers:

$$\begin{array}{r} 48 \\ \times\ 32 \\ \hline 144_20 \\ +\ 9_16 \\ \hline 153_16 \end{array}$$

Try this question. Write it out carefully and work very neatly. 36 × 23

Using efficient written methods for the multiplication of two-digit integers by a two-digit integer

Worksheet 2

Name: _____

Date: _____

Here is another example of multiplying a two-digit integer by another two-digit integer.

```
     84
  ×  36
  ————
   2520   ← Remember: this row shows 84 × 30
 + 504    ← Remember: this row shows 84 × 6
  ————
   3024
```

Here are some questions that you can complete in your exercise book or on a separate piece of paper. Work very neatly using the method shown on this sheet.

1) 46 × 23   2) 52 × 18   3) 73 × 35   4) 98 × 47

5) 82 × 27   6) 63 × 48   7) 94 × 42   8) 77 × 54

You can use this method to work out the following square numbers.

1) 25^2 2) 18^2 3) 36^2 4) 27^2

I can...
I can multiply two-digit integers by a two-digit integer. ☐
I can remember how to work out square numbers. ☐

Using efficient written methods for the multiplication of three-digit integers by a two-digit integer

Teacher's notes

Building on previous learning
Pupils will already have multiplied two-digit and three-digit numbers by two-digit numbers in previous school years but may well have used a grid method. The method used in this unit is the compact method of long multiplication. Some schools may prefer to use an expanded form of long multiplication before this method. Every school needs a clear written policy on calculation methods and when to use them. Before starting this unit check that the children can already:
- use efficient written methods to multiply integers and decimals by a one-digit number.
- use efficient written methods to multiply two-digit integers by a two-digit integer.
- recall quickly multiplication facts up to 10 x 10.

Learning objectives
- Use efficient written methods for the multiplication of three-digit integers by a two-digit integer.
- Solve multi-step problems; choose and use appropriate calculation strategies at each stage.

Learning outcomes
- The children will be able to multiply three-digit integers by a two-digit integer.

Success criteria
Can the children...
... multiply the following questions involving three-digit integers multiply two-digit integers: 345 x 12, 519 x 24, 768 x 45, 814 x 34, 625 x 25, 128 x 64, 256 x 32, 512 x 16?
... use multiplication as part of their strategy for solving a question such as how many days are there altogether in the years 2010, 2011, 2012, 2013, 2014?

Resources needed
- A clear school policy on the systems and methods to be used in recording multiplications both informally and formally
- A display of multiplication tables
- Multiplication grids for pupils who are not able to recall multiplication facts quickly

Opportunities for using and applying the skills
- Solving multi-step problems, and problems involving fractions, decimals and percentages.
- Choosing and using appropriate calculation strategies at each stage, including calculator use. This book is concerned with calculation strategies based on mental work and written work. Calculators are not required for any of the activities in the book.
- Represent and interpret sequences, patterns and relationships involving numbers: pupils will use their understanding of place value to multiply and 'carry' digits.
- Pupils will be able to apply their knowledge of multiplication to problems involving time. As an extension activity you could ask more able pupils to work out how many days old they are, how many hours old they are, etc.

Using efficient written methods for the multiplication of three-digit integers by a two-digit integer

Help at home sheet

Child's name: **Date:**

Dear Parents

At school we follow the National Curriculum and the Primary Framework for mathematics. One aspect of our work in mathematics is the learning of number skills, including using written methods for the multiplication of three-digit whole numbers by two-digit whole numbers. We are keen to involve parents in their children's learning so you may like to help your child by using some of the ideas on this sheet.

National Curriculum

The Primary Framework for mathematics says that Year 5 pupils should:
- use efficient written methods to multiply two-digit and three-digit integers by a two-digit integer.

You could...

... practise multiplications of three-digit integers by two-digit integers with your child using the method outlined here. Notice that we are multiplying by the tens first rather than by the units first – in this way the children are less likely to forget to write a zero in the units column. It would be useful to remind your child that the word 'integer' simply means 'whole number'. To find the answer to a multiplication question such as 526 x 34 the process is just the same as when we multiplied a two-digit number by another two-digit number. We write it out like this:

Step 1: Multiply the 6 units by the 3 tens: 6 x 30 = 180. The 0 is written in the units column, the 8 is written in the tens column and the 1 is written as small as possible below the hundreds:

Step 2: Multiply the 2 tens by the 3 tens: 20 x 30 = 600. This gives 6 for the hundreds column, plus the 1 that was carried from the tens so 7 is written in the hundreds:

Step 3: Multiply the 5 hundreds by the 3 tens: 500 x 30 = 15000. This gives 5 for the thousands column and 1 for the ten thousands column.

Steps 4: Multiply 526 by 4, by multiplying 6 x 4 = 24, then 20 x 4 = 80, then 500 x 4 = 2000:

Step 5: Add the two answers together:

```
    526
  x  34
  15780
 + 2104
  17884
```

Ask your child to use this method to answer the following questions. Make sure that he/she works neatly in an exercise book or on paper and that he/she follows the method exactly as shown in the example.

① 368 x 57   ② 495 x 25   ③ 502 x 23   ④ 620 x 49   ⑤ 999 x 99

You may like to let us know how your child gets on with these activities – if so please return this sheet with any comments on the back.

Using efficient written methods for the multiplication of three-digit integers by a two-digit integer

Worksheet 1

Name: _____

Date: _____

On this page I am going to multiply a three-digit integer by a two-digit integer.

To find the answer to a multiplication question such as 786 x 42 we write it out like this:

```
    786
x    42
```

Step 1: Multiply the 786 by 40:
6 x 40 = 240
80 x 40 = 3200
700 x 40 = 28000

```
    786
x    42
  31440
```

Step 2: Multiply the 786 by 2:
6 x 2 = 12
80 x 2 = 160
700 x 2 = 1400

```
    786
x    42
  31440
   1572
```

Step 3: Add the two answers together to get the final answer:

```
    786
x    42
  31440
+  1572
  33012
```

Here are some questions that you can complete in your exercise book or on a separate piece of paper. Work very neatly using the method shown on this sheet.

1 345 x 12   **2** 519 x 24   **3** 768 x 45   **4** 814 x 34

5 625 x 25   **6** 128 x 64   **7** 256 x 32   **8** 512 x 16

What do you notice about the answers to the last three questions? Why are they like that?

Andrew Brodie: Number Journey for ages 10-11 © A&C Black Publishers Ltd 2008

Using efficient written methods for the multiplication of three-digit integers by a two-digit integer

Worksheet 2

Name: _____

Date: _____

Read this information:

> Every year has approximately 52 weeks. Actually there are 52 weeks and 1 day in most years and there are 52 weeks and 2 days in leap years.

Using the information above, work with a partner to solve these questions:

1. Approximately how many weeks are there in three years?
2. Approximately how many weeks are there in six years?
3. Is your answer to question 2 exactly double the answer to question 1? Do you think it should be?

Read this information:

> In most years there are 365 days. There are 366 days in a leap year. Leap years usually happen every four years. The years 2012, 2016 and 2020 are leap years.

Use the information above to answer the questions on a separate piece of paper. Use multiplication as part of your method and show your working.

1. How many days are there altogether in the years 2010, 2011, 2012, 2013, 2014?
2. How many days have there been altogether since the last day of the year 2002?

I can...
I can multiply three-digit integers by a two-digit integer. ☐
I can use my multiplication skills when solving problems. ☐

Using efficient written methods for the division of integers by a one-digit number (Method 1)

Teacher's notes

Building on previous learning
Pupils may have used written methods for the division of integers by one-digit numbers in Years 4 and 5. They may have used a method of subtracting 'chunks', i.e. multiples of the divisor. In Year 6 many pupils have the confidence to remember multiplication and division facts and also have strong understanding of place value and partitioning. The method introduced in this unit is suitable for these children. Please note that we present a more traditional method on page 00 of this book. You may prefer to use that method or perhaps to use the method in this unit first before introducing that method. Before starting this unit check that the children can already:
- use practical and informal written methods to divide two-digit numbers.
- recall multiplication facts up to 10 x 10.
- use multiplication facts to derive division facts.
- find remainders when dividing within the bounds of the multiplication tables, e.g. 23 ÷ 7 = 3 r 2
- partition three-digit integers into multiples of 100, 10 and 1.

Learning objectives
- Use efficient written methods for the division of integers by one-digit numbers.

Learning outcomes
- The children will be able to divide integers by one-digit numbers in the written format of short division.

Success criteria
Can the children…
… divide three-digit integers by one-digit integers in questions with no remainders, such as: 414 ÷ 6, 355 ÷ 5, 288 ÷ 6, 581 ÷ 7, 567 ÷ 9, 584 ÷ 8?
… divide three-digit integers by one-digit integers in questions which may have remainders, such as: 486 ÷ 5, 323 ÷ 6, 252 ÷ 9, 380 ÷ 8, 600 ÷ 7, 312 ÷ 4?
… divide three-digit integers by one-digit integers in questions where the quotient is greater than 100, such as: 954 ÷ 6, 745 ÷ 5, 928 ÷ 4, 804 ÷ 3, 798 ÷ 2, 861 ÷ 7?

Resources needed
- A clear school policy on the systems and methods to be used in recording divisions both informally and formally. The National Strategies' guidance document recommends the introduction of short division for the end of Year 5 or the beginning of Year 6. In this unit we are presenting the recommended short division method, which can be shortened further to resemble the traditional method. On page 57 we present the traditional method. Your school will need to decide which of these methods to deploy.

Opportunities for using and applying the skills
- Solving multi-step problems, and problems involving fractions, decimals and percentages.
- Represent and interpret sequences, patterns and relationships involving numbers: pupils will use their understanding of place value to divide and 'carry' digits.

Using efficient written methods for the division of integers by a one-digit number (Method 1)

Help at home sheet

Child's name: **Date:**

Dear Parents

At school we follow the National Curriculum and the Primary Framework for mathematics. One aspect of our work in mathematics is the learning of number skills, including developing and using written methods for the division of whole numbers by one-digit numbers. There are lots of methods that can be used for division. The method that we are showing on this sheet is recommended to schools by the National Strategy and is very logical if pupils are confident with multiplication and division facts. We are keen to involve parents in their children's learning so you may like to help your child by using some of the ideas on this sheet.

National Curriculum

The Primary Framework for mathematics says that Year 6 pupils should:
- use efficient written methods to multiply and divide integers and decimals by a one-digit integer.

You could...

... practise divisions with your child using the method outlined here.

To find the answer to a division question such as 392 ÷ 4 we write the question out like this:

$$4\overline{)390 + 2}$$

Ask the question, 'How many fours in 390?' Tell your child that the answer has to be given as a multiple of 10. This gives 90 fours, which is equal to 360, with 30 remaining. The 30 can be combined with the 2 units to give a total of 32. Now ask: 'How many fours in 32?' The answer is 8. So the total answer is 98. Look at how the question is set out:

$$4\overline{)390 + 2} \quad = \quad 4\overline{)360 + 32}^{\,90 + 8}$$

Ask your child to use this method to answer the following questions. Make sure that he/she works neatly in an exercise book or on paper and that he/she follows the method shown in the example.

1) 267 ÷ 3   **2)** 435 ÷ 5   **3)** 574 ÷ 7   **4)** 276 ÷ 4   **5)** 588 ÷ 6

You may like to let us know how your child gets on with these activities – if so please return this sheet with any comments on the back.

Using efficient written methods for the division of integers by a one-digit number (Method 1)

Worksheet 1

Name: _____

Date: _____

On this page I am going to divide by one-digit numbers using short division.

Look at this example.

Step 1: To find the answer to a division question such as 234 ÷ 3 we write the question out like this:

$$3\overline{)230 + 4} =$$

Step 2: Ask the question, 'How many threes in 230?' The answer has to be given as a multiple of 10. The answer to the question is 70, with a remainder of 20, because 70 x 3 = 210 So now we combine the remainder of 20 with the 4 and divide the 24 by 3:

$$3\overline{)230 + 4} = 3\overline{)230 + 4}^{\,70+8}$$

So we can see that 234 ÷ 3 = 78

Use this method to try these questions in your maths book.

① 414 ÷ 6   ② 355 ÷ 5   ③ 288 ÷ 6

④ 581 ÷ 7   ⑤ 567 ÷ 9   ⑥ 584 ÷ 8

Now try these. Watch out, some of them will have a remainder!

① 486 ÷ 5   ② 323 ÷ 6   ③ 252 ÷ 9

④ 380 ÷ 8   ⑤ 600 ÷ 7   ⑥ 312 ÷ 4

Using efficient written methods for the division of integers by a one-digit number (Method 1)

Worksheet 2

Name: _____

Date: _____

Look at this example.

Step 1: To find the answer to a question such as 747 ÷ 3 we write the question out like this:

$$3\overline{)700 + 40 + 7}$$

Notice that we have partitioned the question into hundreds, tens and units because 700 is more than 300. Now, giving your answer as a multiple of 100, how many threes are there in 700? As a multiple of 100, the answer is 200 with 100 remaining because 200 × 3 = 600:

$$3\overline{)700 + 40 + 7} = 3\overline{)600 + 140 + 7}^{\,200}$$

Step 2: Now, giving your answer as a multiple of 10, how many threes are there in 140? As a multiple of 10, the answer is 40 with 20 remaining because 40 × 3 = 120:

$$3\overline{)700 + 40 + 7} = 3\overline{)600 + 140 + 27}^{\,200 + \ 40}$$

Step 3: Now, how many threes are there in 27? The answer is 9:

$$3\overline{)700 + 40 + 7} = 3\overline{)600 + 140 + 27}^{\,200 + \ 40 + \ 9}$$

So 747 ÷ 3 = 249

Use this method to try these questions in your maths book.

- **1** 954 ÷ 6
- **2** 745 ÷ 5
- **3** 928 ÷ 4
- **4** 804 ÷ 3
- **5** 798 ÷ 2
- **6** 861 ÷ 7

I can...
I can use short division to divide three-digit integers by a one-digit integer. ☐
I can find remainders when dividing. ☐

Using efficient written methods for the division of integers by a one-digit number (Method 2)

Teacher's notes

Building on previous learning
The method shown in this unit can be used either as an alternative to Method 1 shown on page 53 or as a natural follow-on to Method 1. In Year 6 many pupils have the confidence to remember multiplication and division facts and also have strong understanding of place value and partitioning. The method introduced in this unit is suitable for these children and consists of the 'traditional' process of short division. Before starting this unit check that the children can already:
- use practical and informal written methods to divide two-digit numbers.
- recall multiplication facts up to 10 x 10.
- use multiplication facts to derive division facts.
- find remainders when dividing within the bounds of the multiplication tables, e.g. 23 ÷ 7 = 3 r 2
- partition three-digit integers into multiples of 100, 10 and 1.

Learning objectives
- Use efficient written methods for the division of integers by one-digit numbers.

Learning outcomes
- The children will be able to divide integers by one-digit numbers in the written format of short division.

Success criteria
- Can the children…
  … use short division to divide three-digit integers by one-digit integers in questions with no remainders, such as: 382 ÷ 2, 748 ÷ 4, 825 ÷ 5, 519 ÷ 3, 496 ÷ 4, 888 ÷ 6?
  … use short division to divide three-digit integers by one-digit integers in questions which may have remainders, such as: 597 ÷ 2, 850 ÷ 4, 678 ÷ 5, 894 ÷ 3, 972 ÷ 7, 940 ÷ 6?

Resources needed
- A clear school policy on the systems and methods to be used in recording divisions both informally and formally. The National Strategies' guidance document recommends the introduction of short division for the end of Year 5 or the beginning of Year 6. Please note that Method 1 on page 00 follows the guidance and uses an alternative form of wording to this unit. However, the method that we present here is quick and efficient and readily transferrable to working with decimals. Your school will need to decide which of these methods to deploy or whether to use both of them.

Opportunities for using and applying the skills
- Solving multi-step problems, and problems involving fractions, decimals and percentages.
- Choosing and using appropriate calculation strategies at each stage, including calculator use. This book is concerned with calculation strategies based on mental work and written work. Calculators are not required for any of the activities in the book.
- Represent and interpret sequences, patterns and relationships involving numbers: pupils will use their understanding of place value to divide and 'carry' digits.

Using efficient written methods for the division of integers by a one-digit number (Method 2)

Help at home sheet

Child's name: **Date:**

Dear Parents
At school we follow the National Curriculum and the Primary Framework for mathematics. One aspect of our work in mathematics is the learning of number skills, including developing and using written methods for the division of whole numbers by one-digit numbers. There are lots of methods that can be used for division. The method that we are showing on this sheet is the traditional form of short division. We are keen to involve parents in their children's learning so you may like to help your child by using some of the ideas on this sheet.

National Curriculum

The Primary Framework for mathematics says that Year 6 pupils should:
- use efficient written methods to multiply and divide integers and decimals by a one-digit integer.

You could...

... practise divisions with your child using the method outlined here.

To find the answer to a division question such as 236 ÷ 4 we write the question out like this:

$$4\overline{)236}$$

Ask the question, 'what's 2 divided by 4?' It can't be done to give a whole number answer so the hundreds column remains empty and the question is then put: 'what's 23 divided by 4?' This gives the answer 5 remainder 3. The 5 is written in the tens column and the 3 is written in front of the 6 to say 36:

$$4\overline{)23^{3}6}^{5}$$

Now ask the question, 'what's 36 divided by 4?' The answer is 9 and should be shown in the units column:

$$4\overline{)23^{3}6}^{59}$$

So 236 ÷ 4 = 59

Ask your child to use this method to answer the following questions. Make sure that he/she works neatly in an exercise book or on paper and that he/she follows the method shown in the example.

1 168 ÷ 3   **2** 455 ÷ 5   **3** 301 ÷ 7   **4** 340 ÷ 4   **5** 432 ÷ 6

You may like to let us know how your child gets on with these activities – if so please return this sheet with any comments on the back.

Using efficient written methods for the division of integers by a one-digit number (Method 2)

Worksheet 1

Name: _____

Date: _____

On this page I am going to divide by one-digit numbers.

Step 1: To find the answer to a division question such as 597 ÷ 3 you can write the question out like this:

$$3\overline{)597}$$

Step 2: Ask the question, 'what's 5 divided by 3?'
    5 ÷ 3 = 1 r 2
So you can put 1 in the hundreds column and carry the 2 to the tens column:

$$3\overline{)5^297}$$ with 1 above

Step 3: Now ask the question, 'what's 29 divided by 3?'
    29 ÷ 3 = 9 r 2
The 9 should be written in the tens column and you should carry the 2 to the units column:

$$3\overline{)5^29^27}$$ with 19 above

Step 4: Now ask the question, 'what's 27 divided by 3?'
    27 ÷ 3 = 9
There is no remainder so you just write the 9 in the units column:

$$3\overline{)5^29^27}$$ with 199 above

So 597 ÷ 3 = 199

Work out the answers to the questions below in your exercise book or on a piece of paper. Work very neatly.

1. 382 ÷ 2
2. 748 ÷ 4
3. 825 ÷ 5
4. 519 ÷ 3
5. 496 ÷ 4
6. 888 ÷ 6

Sometimes there are not enough hundreds to be divided, so the hundreds join with the tens. Look at this example:

We couldn't do 2 ÷ 3 to get an integer answer, so the two hundreds joined the six tens so that we could do 26 ÷ 3.

$$3\overline{)26^27}$$ with 89 above

Try these:

7. 268 ÷ 4
8. 245 ÷ 5
9. 476 ÷ 7

Using efficient written methods for the division of integers by a one-digit number (Method 2)

Worksheet 2

Name: _____

Date: _____

Sometimes the answer will have a remainder.

Step 1: To find the answer to a division question such as 742 ÷ 3 you can write the question out like this:

$$3\overline{)742}$$

Step 2: Ask the question, 'what's 7 divided by 3?'
   7 ÷ 3 = 2 r 1
So you can put 2 in the hundreds column and carry the 1 to the tens column:

$$3\overline{)7^142}$$
(with 2 above)

Step 3: Now ask the question, 'what's 14 divided by 3?'
   14 ÷ 3 = 4 r 2
The 4 should be written in the tens column and you should carry the 2 to the units column:

$$3\overline{)7^14^22}$$
(with 24 above)

Step 4: Now ask the question, 'what's 22 divided by 3?'
   22 ÷ 3 = 7 r 1
Write the 7 in the units column, then write r 1:

$$3\overline{)7^14^22}$$
(with 247 r 1 above)

So 742 ÷ 3 = 247 r 1

Work out the answers to the questions below in your exercise book or on a piece of paper. Work very tidily. Not all of the questions have remainders.

1. 597 ÷ 2
2. 850 ÷ 4
3. 678 ÷ 5
4. 894 ÷ 3
5. 972 ÷ 7
6. 940 ÷ 6

I can...
I can calculate divisions using the short division method. ☐
I can find remainders when dividing. ☐

Using efficient written methods for the division of numbers including decimals by a one-digit number

Teacher's notes

Building on previous learning
Before starting this unit check that the children can already:
- Use short division confidently.
- Recall multiplication facts up to 10 x 10.
- Use multiplication facts to derive division facts.
- Find remainders when dividing within the bounds of the multiplication tables, e.g. 23 ÷ 7 = 3 r 2
- Partition three-digit integers into multiples of 100, 10 and 1.

The method shown in this unit is again the 'traditional' form of short division and follows on naturally from the previous unit.

Learning objectives
- Use efficient written methods for the division of numbers including decimals, by one-digit numbers.

Learning outcomes
- The children will be able to divide numbers including decimals by one-digit numbers in the written format of short division.
- The children will be able to use short division to convert fractions to decimals.

Success criteria
- Can the children…
  … use short division to divide numbers that include decimals, such as:
  5.76 ÷ 2, 7.92 ÷ 4, 6.25 ÷ 5, 9.78 ÷ 3, 4.24 ÷ 4, 8.28 ÷ 6?
  … use short division to convert these fractions to decimals: $\frac{1}{2}, \frac{1}{4}, \frac{3}{4}, \frac{3}{8}, \frac{1}{3}, \frac{5}{8}$?

Resources needed
- A clear school policy on the systems and methods to be used in recording divisions both informally and formally. The National Strategies' guidance document recommends the introduction of short division for the end of Year 5 or the beginning of Year 6. Please note that Method 1 on page 55 follows the guidance and shows an alternative form of wording to that which we are using in this unit. However, the method that we present here is quick and efficient and extends the process shown in the previous unit to the division of decimals. Your school needs to decide which of these methods to deploy or whether to use both of them.

Opportunities for using and applying the skills
- Solving multi-step problems, and problems involving fractions, decimals and percentages.
- Choosing and using appropriate calculation strategies at each stage, including calculator use. This book is concerned with calculation strategies based on mental work and written work. Calculators are not required for any of the activities in the book.
- Represent and interpret sequences, patterns and relationships involving numbers: pupils will use their understanding of place value to divide and 'carry' digits.

Using efficient written methods for the division of numbers including decimals by a one-digit number

Help at home sheet

Child's name: **Date:**

Dear Parents

At school we follow the National Curriculum and the Primary Framework for mathematics. One aspect of our work in mathematics is the learning of number skills, including developing and using written methods for the division of whole numbers and decimals by one-digit numbers. There are lots of methods that can be used for division. The method that we are showing on this sheet is the traditional form of short division, which works very successfully for the division of decimals. We are keen to involve parents in their children's learning so you may like to help your child by using some of the ideas on this sheet.

National Curriculum

The Primary Framework for mathematics says that Year 6 pupils should:
- use efficient written methods to multiply and divide integers and decimals by a one-digit integer.

You could...

... practise divisions with your child using the method outlined here.

To find the answer to a division question such as $2.92 \div 4$ we write the question out like this:

$$4 \overline{) 2.9\,2}$$

Ask the question, 'what's 2 divided by 4?' It can't be done to give a whole number answer so a 0 is written in the units column and the question is then put: 'what's 29 divided by 4?' This gives the answer 7 remainder 1. The 7 is written in the tenths column and the 1 is written in front of the 2 hundredths to say 12:

$$4 \overline{) 2.9\,^1 2}^{\,0.7}$$

Now ask the question, 'what's 12 divided by 4?' The answer is 3 and should be shown in the hundredths column:

$$4 \overline{) 2.9\,^1 2}^{\,0.7\,3} \qquad \text{So } 2.92 \div 4 = 0.73$$

Ask your child to use this method to answer the following questions. Make sure that he/she works neatly in an exercise book or on paper and that he/she follows the method shown in the example. Sometimes, of course, there will not be a zero for the units part of the answer.

❶ $3.65 \div 5$ **❷** $7.68 \div 6$ **❸** $9.56 \div 4$ **❹** $9.59 \div 7$ **❺** $7.95 \div 3$

You may like to let us know how your child gets on with these activities – if so please return this sheet with any comments on the back.

Using efficient written methods for the division of numbers including decimals by a one-digit number

Worksheet 1

Name: _____

Date: _____

On this page I am going to divide a number that has a decimal part, by one-digit numbers.

Step 1: To find the answer to a division question such as 7.05 ÷ 3 we write the question out like this:

$$3\overline{)7.05}$$

Step 2: Ask the question, 'what's 7 divided by 3?'
7 ÷ 3 = 2 r 1
The 2 is written in the units column and the 1 is written in front of the 0 in the tenths column:

$$3\overline{)7.^{1}05}^{\,2}$$

Notice the decimal point on the answer line

Step 3: Now ask the question, 'what's 10 divided by 3?'
10 ÷ 3 = 3 r 1
The 3 is written in the tenths column and the 1 is written in front of the 5 in the hundredths column:

$$3\overline{)7.^{1}0^{1}5}^{\,2.3}$$

Step 4: Now, what's 15 divided by 3?
15 ÷ 3 = 5
There is no remainder so the 5 is written in the hundredths column.

$$3\overline{)7.^{1}0^{1}5}^{\,2.35}$$

So 7.05 ÷ 3 = 2.35

Work out the answers to the questions below in your exercise book or on a piece of paper. Work very tidily.

1) 5.76 ÷ 2   2) 7.92 ÷ 4   3) 6.25 ÷ 5
4) 9.78 ÷ 3   5) 4.24 ÷ 4   6) 8.28 ÷ 6

Using efficient written methods for the division of numbers including decimals by a one-digit number

Worksheet 2

Name: _____

Date: _____

You can use division to change a fraction to a decimal.

Step 1: To change $\frac{1}{8}$ to a decimal you need to work out the top divided by the bottom, that's the numerator divided by the denominator:

$8\overline{)1}$

Write a decimal point then some noughts after the 1:

$8\overline{)1.000}$

Step 2: Now ask the question, 'what's 1 divided by 8?' It can't be done to give a whole number answer so write a 0 in the units column and then ask, 'what's 10 divided by 8?'
$10 \div 8 = 1 \text{ r } 2$
Write the 1 as the answer in the tenths column and write the 2 with the 0 in the hundredths column:

$\begin{array}{r} 0.1 \\ 8\overline{)1.0^200} \end{array}$

Step 3: Now, what's 20 divided by 8?
$20 \div 8 = 2 \text{ r } 4$
Write the 2 as the answer in the hundredths column and write the 4 with the 0 in the thousandths column:

$\begin{array}{r} 0.12 \\ 8\overline{)1.0^20^40} \end{array}$

Step 4: Now, what's 40 divided by 8?
$40 \div 8 = 5$
So write 5 in the thousandths column answer.

$\begin{array}{r} 0.125 \\ 8\overline{)1.0^20^40} \end{array}$

So $\frac{1}{8} = 0.125$

Find the decimal equivalent of each fraction below. You may know some of them already and for those you can just write the answers, but for the others work them out using division. One of the decimals could go on for ever so with this one you should stop at the third decimal place.

1) $\frac{1}{2}$ 2) $\frac{1}{4}$ 3) $\frac{3}{4}$

4) $\frac{3}{8}$ 5) $\frac{1}{3}$ 6) $\frac{5}{8}$

I can...
I can use short division to divide numbers that include decimals. ☐
I can use short division to convert fractions to decimals. ☐